100 Years from Now
Sustaining a Movement for Generations

100 Years from Now invites a truly global conversation on what the Spirit is saying to the churches about God's mission for every nation.

— Dr. Timoteo Gener
President and Professor of Theology, Asian Theological Seminary

Steve's heart for the lost and his passion for discipleship are surpassed only by his love for his Savior and the Church. I believe the perspective given in *100 Years from Now* will strengthen Every Nation to successfully pass the baton from generation to generation and maintain their original, heaven-given mandate.

— Iliafi Esera
General Superintendent, New Zealand Assemblies of God

By all appearances, the prognosis for our culture is not good. If present trends continue, the last of the rich legacy left to us in Christendom will have been squandered within a century. But it need not be. As Steve Murrell reminds us in this must-read book, the power of the Gospel to transform individuals, families, communities, and cultures is irrepressible — if only we would passionately believe it, live it, and apply it.

— George Grant
Pastor of Parish Presbyterian Church,
Author of *Second Fiddles* and *The Wider Diameter of Light*

A friend once challenged me to have a one hundred-year vision. Reading Steve's book explains why every effective leader wants that sort of vision. *100 Years from Now* is the sort of book that leaders will devour. It's a movement book, a leadership book, and a storybook that will leave you both laughing and crying, and hoping and praying, that you, too, will leave a legacy that lasts 100 years from now — or longer. I want every leader I'm discipling to read this book.

— Floyd McClung
Founder, All Nations

I've had the honor of knowing Steve Murrell since his early days in ministry — back when he was a zealous college student with a passion to win the world for Christ. What an incredible journey he has had! Today, he and the men and women he has discipled are transforming nations for Jesus. This book will inspire you to invest your life into what matters most. I pray this book will spark a fresh passion for evangelism in the global church.

— J. Lee Grady
Author and Award-Winning Journalist

Steve so naturally challenges us to broaden the scope of our efforts, while facing the depth of their effects on the future of the world. Join him in these pages as he weaves vision, values, and process into a reality destined for the ages.

— Ralph Moore
Founding Pastor, Hope Chapel (Foursquare Church)

Vast numbers of movements and organizations have begun with an anointing and empowering of the Holy Spirit, only to lose their passion when the founder or leader passed the baton to another generation. While *100 Years from Now* targets the leadership of Every Nation, it speaks to the heart of every leader who wants to grow a work so strong he won't be missed when he's not there. I personally have appreciated Steve Murrell's humility, focus, and willingness to empower a generation of leaders the world over to fulfill the Great Commission and glorify God. Pastor Steve writes with passion, clarity, and purpose.

— Dr. Harold Sala
Founder, Guidelines International

Every decade or so, someone taps into God's heart and writes a landmark book on world evangelization. Steve Murrell has written just such a book for our time. Too often, the Church's thinking is reactionary instead of preemptive. Steve Murrell dares us to embrace and live out a theology embedded in biblical hope. *100 Years from Now* is a challenge and a hopeful vision every believer should embrace.

— David Shibley
Author and Missiologist

As an eyewitness of the phenomenal growth of Every Nation, I saw how a small group of people that applied the biblical principles of discipleship has become one of the most dynamic worldwide ministries today. Steve lived out such principles and now challenges not only their global movement but everyone who are serious in fulfilling the Great Commission to relentlessly implement such principles.

—Efraim Tendero, National Director,
Philippine Council of Evangelical Churches
Executive Director, Philippine Relief and Development Services

100 Years from Now
Sustaining a Movement for Generations

Steve Murrell

DUNHAM
books

DEDICATION

100 Years from Now is dedicated to future
generations of church planters and campus
missionaries who will strategically and
sacrificially take the Gospel to every nation.

*One generation commends your works to
another; they tell of your mighty acts.*
— Psalm 145:4

*It was said among the nations,
"The Lord has done great things for them."*
— Psalm 126:2

100 Years from Now
Copyright © 2013 by Steve Murrell
All rights reserved

For information on sales, licensing, or permissions, contact the publisher:

Dunham Books
63 Music Square East
Nashville, Tennessee 37203
www.dunhamgroupinc.com

Trade Paperback ISBN: 978-1-939447-22-7
Ebook ISBN: 978-1-939447-23-4

Printed in the United States of America

CONTENTS

FOREWORD

What does a real movement look like?

Actual movements are tricky things, but the word has never been more popular. People keep referring to themselves as "a movement for global change," or "a church-planting movement." If we're honest, however, that's usually not the case.

So why do so many people classify themselves as a movement? People want to be a part of one. I recognize that desire because I share it. I am a seeker of movements. I want one. We need one.

Yet only God can create a movement — it takes His divine and sovereign work. But based on my observations in history and around the world today, there do seem to be some patterns related to such movements.

The obvious question is, "What will it take for one to start now?" Here are three things that I believe we need to spark a movement.

First, we need unreasonable men and women. The comfortable do not create movements. Instead, they originate with those who are desperate, demanding something different. Movements come from those who become more committed than they are now. George Bernard Shaw, Irish dramatist and socialist, once said, "The reasonable man adapts himself to the world; the unreasonable one persists in trying to adapt the world to himself. Therefore all progress depends on the unreasonable man." He's right — in a way.

I'd say that when women and men allow their faith to be tamed by the world, they end up with a "nice religion" — and uninterested in the big issues like global evangelization, world poverty, and injustice. That's why I love passionate people. We need more, not less of them.

Christianity needs unreasonable people who are uncomfortable with the status quo and unwilling to be content with the current mode of life and church. We all need a cause bigger than ourselves, which can drive us to action with a holy dissatisfaction.

Second, we need churches that are willing to sacrifice. Seeing the Kingdom as more important than an individual church will take sacrifice, but that's what a movement is about. For so many churches that are simply trying to get by, however, that is an odd thing. Instead of a vision for the Kingdom, they have a vision for survival.

A movement takes churches that so believe in their mission and cause that they are willing to sacrifice for it — financially, congregationally, and corporately. They are willing to give *and* go. Movement churches will sacrifice people to send out missionaries around the world and church planters across the nation.

Everyone wants to be a part of a movement, as long as someone else is paying the price. Everyone loves a movement, as long as it looks great, but costs them little. A true movement will have a steep price, but those who are a part of it will recognize the immeasurable value.

Finally, we need multiplying disciples.

That's so basic it is easy to miss, but it cannot be more essential. The fact is, no disciples are willing to be unreasonable and no churches are willing to sacrifice unless deeply committed disciples are involved.

Discipleship is the DNA of "*movemental* Christianity." It is the basic building block of anything Jesus calls us to do, which is why it is central to the mission of God.

Disciples are unreasonable because they want the world to know of Jesus and to live as those who are changed by the Gospel's power. Disciples demand that their churches sacrifice for greater Gospel good.

No Christian movement can be birthed without discipleship. It is impossible.

So what needs to happen, and what needs to change? Well, there are many things, but let me suggest one big idea for now.

Get dissatisfied.

That's what I love about Steve Murrell's book, *100 Years from Now*, and the ministry of Every Nation. They're dissatisfied, often unreasonable, willing to sacrifice, and focused on discipleship.

That's the stuff of movements.

— **Ed Stetzer**
President, LifeWay Research

HISTORY

- *The Gospel*
- *The Mission*
- *The Values*
- *The Culture*

ONE

100 YEARS FROM NOW

Your story is the greatest legacy that you will leave to your friends. It's the longest-lasting legacy you will leave to your heirs.

— Steve Saint, son of missionary martyr Nate Saint

One generation will commend your works to another; they will tell of your mighty acts.

— David (Psalm 145:4)

"HEY DAD, YOU WON'T BELIEVE where I am."

William, my oldest son, was whispering into his cell phone. I could barely hear him. He was calling from England where he was enrolled in a one-semester exchange program at Oxford University's Wycliffe Hall.

"Right now I'm sitting in a pew at St. Aldates, the same church John and Charles Wesley and George Whitfield attended when they were students here almost three hundred years ago. This place is amazing!"

Lessons from a One Thousand-Year-Old Church

Four years later, William was back at Oxford working on his master's degree in medieval history, and this time, my wife, Deborah, and I got a chance to visit him. Like all historians, William is a semi-pro tour guide; Deborah is a tour junkie. Our Oxford tour included the Bodleian Library, Christ Church Meadow, and famous pubs, but St. Aldates was the highlight. The church was established over one thousand years ago, and the building is over nine hundred years old.

While the old church's architecture is beautiful, its history is rich, and its membership role is filled with world-changers, I will never forget the small, nondescript stone plaque listing the name of every pastor who has led St. Aldates during its illustrious one thousand-year history. The list was surprisingly short. St. Aldates' pastors tend to stay faithful in one pulpit until they die. Maybe this life-long pastoral commitment is one reason St. Aldates is still a thriving faith community ten centuries later.

As William moved our tour to another part of the magnificent building, I found myself frozen in front of that list of pastors' names carved in stone, pondering how a local church could continuously minister in the same town for one thousand years. Every European town I have visited has an old church *building* still standing, but how many church *communities* are still alive and well after a millennium?

As I read the names on the plaque, I thought about other movements that have endured the test of time. While attending Oxford and St. Aldates in the early 1700s, the Wesley brothers got involved in "holy clubs" that were designed to disciple students. Within a few years, the members of this fledgling group of disciples were mockingly called "Methodists" because of their methodical approach to small group discipleship. Today, the World Methodist Council includes seventy-five million people in seventy-six denominations in 132 nations. I doubt that when John and Charles started those "holy clubs" they expected to have seventy-five million followers three hundred years later, but they did something that created and sustained a movement. Their "Methodist" baton was successfully passed from generation to generation, nation to nation, century to century.

The Perfect Storm and the Hundred-Year Prayer Meeting

John Wesley would be an unknown, obscure footnote in Oxford history, if not for his close encounter with Moravian missionaries during his failed mission adventure to the Colony of Georgia. In his journal, Wesley describes his encounter with Moravians who were on his ship while crossing the Atlantic Ocean during a perfect storm:

Sunday, January 25, 1736. In the midst of the psalm wherewith their service began, the sea broke over, split the main-sail in pieces, and poured in between the decks, as if the great deep had already swallowed us up. A terrible screaming began among the English. The Germans (Moravians) calmly sung on. I asked one of them afterwards, "Were you not afraid?" He answered, "I thank God, no." I asked, "But were not your women and children afraid?" He replied, mildly, "No; our women and children are not afraid to die."

This unexpected meeting with joyful Christians who were not afraid to die caused Wesley to seek out Moravians while on mission in Georgia and when he returned to England. He even visited them in Germany seeking answers as to why they remained so peaceful in the face of death. Eventually, Wesley found the answer: salvation by grace through faith in Christ alone.

Who were these Moravians who had such an impact on Wesley? They were actually the spiritual descendants of a movement started in the fourteenth century by John Hus. By the early 1700s, they were a small, struggling community of about three hundred in Saxony, the eastern edge of Germany, but they would eventually impact the world. A young German noble named Nikolaus Ludwig von Zinzendorf was their benefactor, and would soon become their leader. On August 27, 1727, twenty-four men and twenty-four women volunteered to pray one hour a day for the people around the world "for whom no one cared." In a few decades, thousands of Moravians would become missionaries to those people "for whom no one cared" in some of the most dangerous and remote places on the planet. That twenty-four-hour-a-day prayer meeting lasted uninterrupted for more than one hundred years. Zinzendorf died in 1760, but the prayer meeting and mission movement continued without him. Real leaders dream of this — a movement that outlives them, a movement that does not skip a beat when they die, a movement that no longer needs them.

Thinking About the Next Hundred Years

For most of us who are conditioned to live in the moment, it's almost impossible to relate to St. Aldates and think about the one thousand-year implications of our decisions, or even the Methodists and the three hundred year impact of decisions. But maybe we can learn from the praying Moravians how to think about the one hundred-year implications. If they can have a prayer meeting that lasts for one hundred years, then we should be able to make decisions that last that long.

My friend, Russ Austin, the pastor of Southpoint Community Church in Jacksonville, Florida, and the regional director of Every Nation North America, often challenges pastors to think about the hundred-year domino effect of actions and decisions. His favorite leadership question is: "If we make this decision now, how will it impact us in one hundred years? And, if we drop the ball on this (project, value, relationship, doctrine), what will we be as a result in one hundred years?" Russ is convinced that we will make better decisions if we think long-term. I agree with Russ.

While I have always tried to think long-term as a pastor, church planter, missiologist, and leader, I fear that I often get stuck in the present and miss the future implications of my decisions. While staring at the names of one thousand years of St. Aldates pastors, I thought about Every Nation. Would we even exist in one thousand years or one hundred years? Would our future leaders stay faithful to the mission, vision, values, culture, and doctrines that gave birth to Every Nation? Would the things we're passionate about today still matter in a decade or a century?

I guess the answer depends on how successfully we pass the baton to future generations.

Worse Than Dropping the Baton

Many years ago, I was a runner. Not a jogger or a marathoner. A runner. My older brother, Jim, was also a runner. In 1975, Jim was a high school senior; I was a sophomore. Being the fastest man on our track team, Jim ran the 100, and usually won. I was fast enough to barely make the 4x100 relay team. Halfway through the season, in an insignificant track meet, Coach decided to put me in the 100 along with Jim, just to see what would happen. Who can resist a little brother-against-brother competition? Since all eyes were on Jim, I approached the starting line with no pressure and no expectations. Ten seconds after the gun sounded, the unexpected happened. I not only beat my big brother, I won the race. Jim came in second. No one was more surprised than me, except maybe Jim and Coach.

Thirty minutes later, we lined up for the 4x100 relay. Jim ran the first leg; I ran the second. Jim shot out of the blocks like Usain Bolt running from a hungry cheetah. He left our opponents in his dust like they were in slow motion. He was flying, but something was not right. As he rounded the curve for the handoff, I squinted my eyes and couldn't believe what I saw, or rather, what I didn't see. *Where's the baton? Jim, you're supposed to have a baton!*

Last summer, at my son's wedding, we were laughing about childhood memories, including that race, and Jim told me that he was so mad about losing the 100 to his little brother, that he completely forgot to pick up the baton and just left it there on the starting line. I'm not sure when he realized he had forgotten the baton, but as he approached me for the handoff, he was half yelling, half laughing, and furiously waving his hands, "I forgot the baton, just run!" So we slapped hands and I ran, with our invisible baton. I then passed that imaginary baton to the third runner who passed it to our fourth runner. Of course, we were disqualified because running with an imaginary baton doesn't count. It didn't matter that our team was the fastest on the track. All that mattered was that we failed to pass the baton. We didn't drop it. We left it at the starting line.

I sent an early draft of this chapter to my brother to make sure he remembered the story the way I wrote it. Here's his response:

The story is essentially true as recorded. My memory of it is no different than yours, unfortunately. However, it's a very good example of how "team" is more important than "individual" success. A few life lessons from remembering that single embarrassing event are still with me today. First, it's the only time in my life I've ever run one hundred yards in less than ten seconds. I just wasn't fast enough to beat your 9.8 that day. God has a way of humiliating those who take pride in their own abilities. Second, our team finished one and two in a field of eight! But I was too self-absorbed to celebrate the accomplishment. In the relay, I should have been focusing on another victory for the team rather than trying to avenge my personal humiliation from the race before. The baton is what a relay race is all about. Without it, we all just run in vain.

Every few years, church and ministry leaders embrace their mortality, realize they won't live forever, and start talking about "passing the baton" to the next generation. Old leaders get obsessed with succession. They show each other videos of Olympians dropping the baton and being disqualified. They preach sermons about the importance of not dropping the baton. They hire Harvard-trained consultants to write succession plans that only Harvard-trained consultants can decipher. Bloggers blog about succession plans and baton-passing. Preachers preach about succession plans and baton-passing. Intercessors intercede about succession plans and baton-passing. Then, we all regain our sanity and go back to business as usual, or to the latest recycled get-big-quick idea of the week.

During the baton-passing frenzy, no one seems to ask or know exactly what the baton is that we are supposed to pass to the succeeding generations.

The Whole Point of This Book

This book is not about how to build a baton-passing succession plan. Making the handoff and passing the baton is the simple part. All that is required is to put the baton in the hand of the next runner, let go, and then get out of the way and cheer. It's not complicated.

These pages are about the baton itself. We can create a great succession plan to pass the baton, but it's all for nothing if we leave the baton laying somewhere near the starting line or if we're confused about what baton we're supposed to pass. The following pages will attempt to answer one important question: What is the Every Nation baton? Here's a quick four-part answer to that question.

1. **The Gospel.** The most important baton we pass to the next generation is the Gospel of Jesus Christ. In *Christian Theology*, Millard Erickson describes the Gospel as "the one factor that gives basic shape to *everything* the church does, the element that lies at the heart of *all* its functions." In other words, if we drop the Gospel baton or leave it at the starting line, *everything* else we do in ministry is a waste of time. Consider what Paul said about passing the Gospel baton: "I want to remind you of the Gospel I preached to you . . . By this Gospel you are saved . . . For what I received *I passed on* to you as of first importance: that Christ died for our sins according to the Scriptures, that he was buried, that he was raised on the third day" (1 Corinthians 15:1–4). For Paul, nothing was more important than passing the Gospel to the next generation. In his book, *God's Not Dead*, Rice Broocks summarizes the Gospel. He writes, "The Gospel is the good news that God became man in Jesus Christ. He lived the life we should have lived; He then died the death we should have died. Three days later He rose from the dead, proving that He is the Son of God and offering the gift of salvation to everyone who will repent and believe the Gospel." Chapter 11 will talk more about the Gospel.

2. **Mission.** What is mission and why do we need it? In his book, *The Call*, author Os Guinness describes the power of mission: "Deep in our hearts, we all want to find and fulfill a purpose bigger than ourselves. Only such a larger purpose can inspire us to heights we know we could never reach on our own." How we live out the implications of the Gospel and how we live for something bigger than ourselves are summarized in Every Nation's mission statement: *To honor God by establishing Christ-centered, Spirit-empowered, socially responsible churches and campus ministries in every nation.* This mission statement will be broken down into seven short phrases and covered in chapters 3–9.

3. **Values.** If our mission describes *what* we're called to do, our core
   values describe *how* we do what we do. Kevin York serves as the executive director of Every Nation Churches & Ministries. He's one of
   the most brilliant church consultants I know. Kevin constantly says
   that clearly defined and simply articulated values are vital church
   leadership tools. He notes that "core values are the bull's-eye. When
   we aim at our values, we will also hit our vision and mission." Chapters 10–14 will explain the five Every Nation core values: Lordship,
   evangelism, discipleship, leadership, and family. These big five are
   the core values of our global movement of churches, but are not
   necessarily the core values of a particular local church. Some Every
   Nation churches have *adopted* these five exactly as stated. Others
   have slightly *adapted* them by adding to the five or by contextualiz-
   ing the terminology in a way that makes sense in their local context.
   Your local church may use other qualities in its core value statement, but as a global movement, Every Nation embraces these five.

4. **Culture.** This aspect of the baton is a bit elusive, but vitally important. A couple of years ago, I wrote a book, *WikiChurch,* about
   the Victory-Manila discipleship *process.* A year later, my colleague,
   Joey Bonifacio, wrote a book, *The Lego Principle*, about the Victory-
   Manila discipleship *culture.* Process and culture are both important. Neither is effective without the other. Many have attempted to
   copy a discipleship process, but without a discipleship culture, the
   process is like a muscle car with no fuel. Structure and process are
   important, but for us to be who God has called us to be and to do
   what God has called us to do, we must understand and embrace the
   Every Nation culture. Chapters 15–18 will explain four ingredients
   of our unique culture: vision, generosity, diversity, and sacrifice.
   No matter where in the world you are, if you're in an Every Nation
   church or campus ministry, you will experience these four aspects
   of our culture. Some people visit Every Nation and are repelled by
   one or all four aspects of our culture; other people are attracted to
   them. Both reactions are good.

The Hundred-Year Question

Every Nation is only twenty years old at this writing. In a few short years, we've seen and done a lot. We've made our share of mistakes, and we've learned countless life lessons that can only be learned through experience. Hopefully, future generations will learn from our victories and from our defeats. We are eternally grateful to God for the privilege of being part of His plan for His planet. More than anything, the old dudes in my generation desperately desire to build in such a way that future generations will not have to tear down what we built in order to obey God.

I don't know if Wesley or Zinzendorf or the original founders of St. Aldates asked themselves the hundred-year question, but history shows us what actually happened one hundred years later and beyond because of their lives and ministries. Each chapter in this book will end with some hundred-year questions. Here are the first.

What will Every Nation become in the next one hundred years if we forget our mission, values, and culture, or if we compromise the Gospel? On the other hand, if we are faithful to the Gospel, and if we successfully transfer our mission, values, and culture to the next generation, how will the nations be impacted by the year 2094, when Every Nation celebrates its one-hundredth anniversary?

TWO

WHY WE'RE
BETTER TOGETHER

Friendship is essentially a partnership.

— Aristotle

Two are better than one, because they have a good return for their labor.

— Solomon (Ecclesiastes 4:9)

IN 1982, DEBORAH AND I were newly married campus missionaries living the dream, serving the students of Mississippi State University in the sleepy town of Starkville, Mississippi. Two years later, we were campus missionaries serving Filipino students in Manila's bustling University Belt. Starkville's 1984 population: about twelve thousand. Metro Manila's 1984 population: almost twelve million. To say we were in a different culture would be the understatement of the decade. More like a different planet!

In June of 1984, we went to Manila for what was billed as a one-month summer mission trip. At the end of that month, we were left behind and ended up living in the Philippines for the next few decades. That's why we think of ourselves as accidental missionaries.

The Longest Month in the History of Time

All three of our sons were born and raised in the Philippines. Most of our best memories happened in the Philippines. And many of our life-long friends are Filipinos. When my Every Nation job responsibilities

expanded in 2006, we began splitting time between Manila and Nashville, back and forth across the ocean every six to eight weeks — twen-
ty-first century commuting.

Sometimes we're not really sure how the past twenty-nine years
happened, but here's my best summary. In 1984, my good friend, Rice
Broocks, was leading a team of American college students on a campus
ministry mission trip to Manila, Philippines, and Seoul, South Korea.
Six weeks before the departure date, Rice called and asked if Deborah
and I would help lead the team of sixty-five clueless summer missionaries. As campus missionaries in a small Southern town, we had nothing better to do during summer break, so we signed up, fast-tracked
new passports, and prayed to God for airline ticket money. God answered our prayers and provided the money. We flew to Asia thinking
we would be back in Mississippi in a couple of months. Little did we
know, God had other plans. Sometimes when I think about our never-
ending "summer mission trip," I wonder what Peter experienced that
caused him to write, "with the Lord a day is like a thousand years, and
a thousand years are like a day." Maybe Peter was left behind on a summer mission trip too.

While in the Philippines, we dedicated ourselves to campus ministry. Deborah and I would wake up early each morning, pray, read the
Bible, walk to the bus stop, ride a bus to Manila's University Belt, spend
the day engaging Filipino students with the Gospel, then commute
back to our high-rise apartment. That routine was repeated Monday
through Friday. On Saturday, I would prepare for Sunday, which included preaching and discipleship activities all day, and then we would
start all over on Monday. It would be many years before we grasped
the concept of a day off. Eventually, the students we reached graduated,
got jobs, got married, and raised kids. Eventually, their kids graduated, got jobs, got married, and raised kids of their own. And I got old.
Deborah didn't. Somewhere during our journey, I think she discovered
the Filipino fountain of youth, but she refuses to tell me where it is.
In the meantime, those original 180 Filipino students we reached in
Manila's University Belt in 1984, gradually grew into a pretty big multi-
site, multi-generational, Christ-centered, Spirit-empowered, socially

responsible church that meets in sixteen Manila locations. That church is now called Victory, and it has planted churches in sixty Philippine cities and has sent and funded Filipino cross-cultural church planters to over two dozen nations, including China, the United Arab Emirates, Bangladesh, Nepal, Vietnam, Cambodia, and others.

But all was not well. Across the ocean, the ministry that sent us to the Philippines self-destructed six years after we landed in Manila, and we suddenly found ourselves with no covering, no sending agency, and almost no financial support. In spite of ministry problems overseas in America, our Filipino church continued to grow and expand all over Metro Manila. It continued to equip and empower campus missionaries. It continued to plant new churches in the Philippine provinces. And it continued to send and support Filipino missionaries all over Asia. But we knew something was missing. We were not at peace doing ministry alone. Let me try to explain what I mean by alone.

Previously, we had been part of a campus ministry and church-planting organization with a worldwide vision, something that was much larger than a local church and its outreach. At that stage in our lives, Deborah and I felt that rather than leading a worldwide movement, we needed to be part of one. I have never really wanted to lead anything, except for my sons' Little League baseball teams. But God has never consulted me about His calling for my life.

Divine Reconnection

Six years after the demise of the ministry and mission agency that sent us to the Philippines, I received a call from Rice that would change our lives. Every decade or so, I get a call like that from him. Rice called to ask if he and an old friend, Phil Bonasso, could crash at my house in Manila for a couple of nights on their way to Singapore and Malaysia.

Rice and Phil's Asian adventure was a response to a "Macedonian call" from a friend of a friend asking them to consider assisting two new church-planting opportunities in Asia. I'll never forget that late night in my house in Manila. Rice and Phil were talking about the open doors in Kuala Lumpur and Singapore, and then one of them said, "We need to plant churches in those cities."

I responded, "Who is 'we?' There is no 'we.' There is only you, and you, and me." In 1989, when Maranatha Campus Ministries ended and we all went our separate ways, any semblance of "we" had abruptly ended.

I can't remember the whole conversation, but by the time Rice and Phil left my house, there was a "we" that the three of us agreed to call Morning Star International. God had connected us together for the purpose of "church planting, campus ministry, and world missions." Phil and I agreed to join our ministries together if Rice would take the lead. We never imagined anyone would want to join with us. We simply wanted to plant new churches, not gather existing churches. To our surprise, as soon as Rice and Phil landed in the USA a week later, old friends started calling to ask if they could join our little church-planting group. A few years later, we changed our name to Every Nation, but we never changed our commitment to church planting, campus ministry, and world missions.

Better Together

When God reconnected Rice, Phil, and me that night in Manila, it was not because we were all struggling and failing. Quite the contrary — all three of us were leading what most people would consider growing and successful ministries. Every Nation came about because the three of us believed we could accomplish more together than apart. We believed we could be better together.

About 2,500 years ago, the apostate Israelites were attacked by the evil Babylonians. The best and brightest young men were dragged from Jerusalem to Babylon. Away from faith and family for the first time, no one would know if these teenaged Jews compromised and experimented with sins they would never dare try at home.

But "Daniel resolved not to defile himself" (Daniel 1:8). He refused to compromise. He also refused to face these new temptations alone. Here's what he said to the Babylonian officials who were offering all kinds of temptations: "Please test your *servants* for ten days: Give *us* nothing but vegetables to eat and water to drink. Then compare *our* appearance with that of the young men who eat the royal food, and treat your *servants* in accordance with what you see" (Daniel 1:12–13).

Notice the plural words in the above passage: *servants, us, our.* We know that Daniel resolved not to compromise, but we have no account of Shadrach, Meshach, and Abednego making the same stand. It seems that as Daniel took his no-compromise leap of faith, he simultaneously pushed his friends off the high board and into the deep end without their consent.

Do you have friends who push, pull, or drag you deeper into God's plan for your life? I do. Fortunately Shadrach, Meshach, and Abednego had Daniel. And the four of them were better together.

Here's how the first chapter of their Babylonian adventure ends: "In every matter of wisdom and understanding about which the king questioned *them,* he found *them* ten times better than all the magicians and enchanters in his whole kingdom" (Daniel 1:22).

They were not only better together; they were "ten times better" together!

Four Reasons We're Better Together

More than 350 years before Daniel and his friends helped each other become ten times better in Babylon, King Solomon recognized and wrote about the same principle.

> Again I saw something meaningless under the sun: There was a man all alone; he had neither son nor brother. There was no end to his toil, yet his eyes were not content with his wealth. "For whom am I toiling," he asked, "and why am I depriving myself of enjoyment?" This too is meaningless — a miserable business! Two are better than one, because they have a good return for their labor: If either of them falls down, one can help the other up. But pity anyone who falls and has no one to help them up. Also, if two lie down together, they will keep warm. But how can one keep warm alone? (Ecclesiastes 4:7–12)

This guy was successful, hard-working, and wealthy, but he was miserable because he was alone. He had no son coming behind him, and he had no brother walking beside him. He had plenty of money but no friends. In the next four verses, he gives four reasons why two are better than one, explaining why life in a community makes us all better.

1. **Increased productivity.** *Two are better than one, because they have a good return for their labor.* Maybe Jesus sent His disciples out two-by-two rather than as lone rangers because He knew that by working together, they would have a good return for their labor.

2. **Increased protection.** *If either of them falls down, one can help the other up. But pity anyone who falls and has no one to help them up.* Falling down does not have to be fatal. We have increased safety and protection when we do life, mission, and ministry together because someone is there to help us up when we're knocked down.

3. **Increased passion.** *Also, if two lie down together, they will keep warm. But how can one keep warm alone?* Left to myself, I would probably be lukewarm or cold most of the time, but thankfully, I am surrounded by people who have more passion for Jesus and His mission than I do. They add fuel to my fire, especially when it starts to flicker.

4. **Increased power.** *Though one may be overpowered, two can defend themselves. A cord of three strands is not quickly broken.* There is power in unity and in community. Jesus set the example when He invited Peter, James, and John to pray with Him in the Garden of Gethsemane. If Jesus did not face His darkest hour alone, then we probably should not either.

The Hundred-Year Question

Sometimes I wonder how things would have turned out if Deborah and I had attempted to do life and ministry like the preacher in Ecclesiastes, *all alone with neither son nor brother.* It's scary to think where I would be today without all my amazing friends who make me a better man and minister.

If we decide to walk alone and resist or neglect God-given relationships, what will happen to us in the next one hundred years? On the other hand, if we allow God to connect us in life-giving ministry partnerships with other individuals and churches, what could be accomplished in the next one hundred years?

MISSION

- *To honor God by establishing Christ-centered, Spirit-empowered, socially responsible churches and campus ministries in every nation.*

THREE

THE ULTIMATE MOTIVE

Man's chief end is to glorify God, and to enjoy him forever.

— Westminster Shorter Catechism

You were bought at a price. Therefore honor God with your body.

— Apostle Paul (1 Corinthians 6:20)

FROM THE MOMENT Rice, Phil, and I felt God calling us to work together, we knew He wanted us to focus on campus ministry, church planting, and world missions. In time, that three-fold focus evolved into our mission statement:

> *We exist to honor God by establishing Christ-centered, Spirit-empowered, socially responsible churches and campus ministries in every nation.*

Chapters 3–9 will attempt to explain and illustrate each part of the Every Nation mission. I will start by looking at the most important part of our mission — honoring God. But first I want to share a short story.

My Mission Trip to Paradise

The summer of 1980 was my first overseas mission trip. This mission adventure was not to the jungles of South America, to the deserts of North Africa, nor to the mountains of Central Asia. Those would come later. After months of praying, fasting, and wrestling with the will of God, I finally said yes to the call. Actually, it wasn't that difficult to hear a "Macedonian call" to be a summer missionary in paradise. This sum- mer mission opportunity was targeting the University of Hawaii. That's right, Hawaii. I figured somebody had to do it; why not me?

So as soon as spring semester finished, I got busy painting houses for six weeks to earn enough money to fund my Hawaii mission trip. I worked hard, saved my money, and God provided. Funny how hard work and disciplined saving can result in God's provision.

About a dozen of us landed at the Honolulu International Airport that summer. After a full day of evangelism training that included at least five minutes of cross-cultural teaching, we were still clueless, but that didn't stop us. We hit the campus with white legs shining and black Bibles blazing. The results were underwhelming. Eventually, de- spite our best efforts, some students actually responded positively to the Gospel and started a life-long walk with Jesus.

After two weeks of campus evangelism, our team leader gave us a day off. Apparently there's a beach in Hawaii.

Our team leader was a former sailor who was out of the military, but the military was still in him. He ran prayer meetings, Bible studies, and lunch like he was running a battleship during a war. This kind of atmosphere in an outreach was neither fun nor productive. A little joy might have helped. But this was a mission trip, and apparently mission trips are not supposed to be fun. So we saluted and soldiered on.

That Does Not Honor God

This guy was super-disciplined. He was never late. And he let us know that we would never be late as long as were on his island. He was quick to cheer our victories but had no hesitation pointing out our mistakes. We were a bunch of college kids, full of zeal and the Holy Spirit, and a lot like what they refer to as "loose cannons on the deck." Our tardi- ness, lack of discipline, and frequent mistakes were corrected daily by our drill-sergeant team leader.

There was, however, another side to him. And from that other side of him I learned a life lesson I hope I never forget. Every word of cor- rection was wrapped around the words: "That attitude does not honor God," or, "Those words do not please the Lord." There was an equal amount of encouragement along the lines of what did, in fact, please and honor God. No matter what we did, right or wrong (and we did a lot of both), it provoked a response that was expressed in the context of what did or did not honor God.

Looking back on that summer, I think some of the corrections might have been things that simply displeased him and didn't bother the Lord at all. Nonetheless, his constant appeal to what did or did not honor God helped change my thinking. Since that summer over three decades ago, I have been obsessed with finding out what pleases and honors God.

We Exist to Honor God

Four years after my Hawaiian mission adventure, Deborah and I were on another summer mission trip, this time to plant a church in the Philippine Islands. After thirty days of evangelistic outreach, by default, it was looking more and more like we were about to be left behind as the team prepared to depart from Manila.

I vividly remember the day I sat down at my Dunkin' Donuts "office" in the heart of Manila's University Belt to write out the mission statement for this one-month-old Filipino church. On a Dunkin' Donuts napkin, I scribbled the first and most important words that came to mind: *We exist to honor God.* The words that came next have evolved numerous times over the years, but the "honor God" part has always been the unchanging anchor.

About ten years after I scribbled that Dunkin' Donuts mission statement, Rice, Phil, and I were having that serendipitous mission moment at my house when God joined our ministries to form Every Nation. We had no disagreement about what would be the top priority of our new mission: *We exist to honor God.* God's honor was and always will be the Every Nation starting line. It will also always be our plumb line and our finish line.

More Than Verbal Honor

While I type these words, I'm in my Manila apartment, a couple of blocks from our Every Nation building. It's Monday afternoon, Philippine time. Super Bowl XLVII ended a couple of hours ago. It used to feel weird watching the Super Bowl (American football championship) live early Monday morning rather than Sunday afternoon, but after so many years, it now feels normal. The Baltimore Ravens won. Watching the spectacle from this side of the world reminded me that it's not uncommon to hear people give God a little verbal honor. As always after American sporting events, the winning players gave post-game shout-outs to God. It's always interesting to watch famous athletes drop F-bombs, and then point to heaven and thank God. Of course, the coaches constantly have God's name on their lips, not exactly in an honorable way. And then there's the halftime extravaganza. This time, as usual, the internationally popular recording artist ended her scantily-clad lingerie pole-dance routine with the ubiquitous "God bless you!" It's indeed common in our culture to honor God with our lips. But do empty words really honor God?

In the last book in the Old Testament, God speaks about honor: "A son honors his father and a servant his master. If I am a Father, where is the honor due me? If I am a Master, where is the respect due me?" (Malachi 1:6). God deserves and expects honor. Real honor must be more than words. We should honor God in the way we do what we do. It is possible to do ministry in a way that honors God, and in a way that dishonors Him. We can take up offerings in ways that honor God, and also in ways that do not. We can build buildings, evangelize the world, disciple the nations, even care for the poor — all in ways that please God or in ways that do not. Contrary to what many suppose, it doesn't matter if God seems to be blessing an initiative. He may bless something that does not particularly please Him. Remember, He causes the rain to fall on both the just and the unjust, and I am pretty sure that He really doesn't like injustice. Overflowing church attendance or bank accounts don't necessarily mean what we are doing, or how we are doing it, are pleasing to God.

When we say that Every Nation exists to honor God, we mean it in every way. We desire to honor God by being faithful to believe and obey His Word. We also want to honor Him in our motivation and methods. And, we hope to honor God in our private lives, in the deepest recesses and darkest corners of our hearts and minds.

Legalism Does Not Honor God

God, in all His awesome power, is a personal God who loves with infinite love. In no sense does He love a little bit. God's love is full-throttled, unconditional, undiluted, and sacrificial. And because of His steadfast love for us, the Holy Spirit is attentive to our thoughts, our words, and our actions. His Spirit is distressed when we're distressed. He's also grieved when we turn our attention to things that don't honor Him. The prophet Isaiah wrote, "In all their distress he too was distressed, and the angel of his presence saved them . . . Yet they rebelled and grieved his Holy Spirit" (Isaiah 63:9–10).

This is where honoring God gets down to the heart. It's also where it takes on a very practical application. Living a life in pursuit of God's honor means that we're always aware, always mindful, and always sensitive to the presence and person of the Holy Spirit — that we desire to please the Lord in our attitude, our actions, and our words. As I heard over and over on my summer mission trip to Hawaii, "Does this please and honor the Lord?" Honoring the Lord is not an institutional policy, but a moment-by-moment awareness of the presence of God. It is not a doctrine preached only from the pulpit, but a mindset in people whose hearts are tuned toward the Holy Spirit and sensitive to what pleases Him and what does not.

I am painfully aware that people like us, passionate in our desire to please and honor the Lord, have a tendency to run the train off the tracks. What begins as a passionate personal encounter with Christ quickly becomes a growing list of well-intended rules and regulations. Legalism eventually replaces dynamic spiritual life, and honoring God is replaced by a set of rules. A group of Pharisees, religious professionals who were famous for this kind of thing, once approached Jesus and criticized Him for breaking their precious religious traditions. Jesus responded by quoting from the prophet Isaiah: "You hypocrites! Isaiah was right when he prophesied about you: 'These people honor me with their lips, but their hearts are far from me. They worship me in vain; their teachings are merely human rules'" (Matthew 15:7–9).

The Hundred-Year Question

We are not the first movement to wrestle with what it means to honor God. Almost four hundred years ago, English and Scottish theologians sought to live all of life to please God. They penned the *Westminster Catechism* to instruct future generations on how to honor God. The catechism's first question is its most important: "What is the chief end of man?" The answer: "Man's chief end is to glorify God, and to enjoy him forever." Both *chief ends* of that answer are equally important. God is not honored by legalistically following a set of rules, but by a passionate pursuit of His glory and by enjoying Him forever.

What are the one hundred-year implications if the honor of God is no longer our ultimate issue, and we become motivated by what will make us popular or big? On the other hand, if we make honoring God our ultimate motive, our starting line, our plumb line, and our finish line, what could Every Nation become in the next one hundred years?

FOUR

THE BORN SUPREMACY

*Truth never becomes clear as long as we assume that
each of us, individually, is the center of the universe.*
— Thomas Merton

*He is the head of the body, the church; he is the
beginning and the firstborn from among the dead, so
that in everything he might have the supremacy.*
— Apostle Paul (Colossians 1:18)

SINCE EVERY NATION EXISTS *to honor God by establishing Christ-
centered, Spirit-empowered, socially responsible churches and campus
ministries in every nation,* we have to ask, what does it mean to be
Christ-centered? Let's start by looking at heaven, which is certainly
Christ-centered.

Here's how the apostle John described his vision of heaven: "Then I
saw a Lamb, looking as if it had been slain, standing *in the center* of the
throne, encircled by the four living creatures and the elders" (Revelation 5:6). In heaven, Jesus, the Lamb of God, is not a side issue; He is
front and center.

While having his heavenly vision, John got to listen to the angels
and a "great multitude that no one could count" singing and shouting
for joy. Here's part of what they sang and shouted: "The Lamb *at the
center* of the throne will be their shepherd" (Revelation 7:17). Again,
Jesus, the Lamb of God, is at the center. That's heaven, but what about
earth? What about the Church? Jesus taught His disciples to pray "your

kingdom come, your will be done on earth as it is in heaven" (Matthew 6:10). If Jesus is the center in heaven, then certainly He should be the center in His Church on earth. But, sadly, too often, He is not.

Losing Our Center

Have you ever lost something valuable? Seventeen years ago, my wife lost her engagement ring. Technically, it's not lost since we know where it is, but it might as well be lost because we'll never see it again. The South China Sea is just too deep. Long story. The replacement was an upgrade, so everyone was happy.

I once lost something much more valuable and irreplaceable than a ring. I lost our oldest son. We were on a family vacation, and we rented bikes to ride through the paved trails in the woods. William was ten and James was eight, so they got to ride. Jonathan was six, not quite ready for the big-boy trails in the woods, so we left him with his mother.

When you raise three sons, competition is always part of the mix. The activity is irrelevant. So after a leisurely ride through the woods to the waterfall, it was time to head back. Someone suggested we race back to the bike rental hut. Game on.

William took off like he was in the *Tour de France* (minus the performance enhancers and corporate sponsors). Since there was no way his brother could keep up the pace, I slowed down so as not to leave my middle son behind us in the woods. William was quickly out of sight. When James and I arrived back at the bike barn, we figured William had already returned his bike. But the desk worker insisted that he had not seen my son since we all peddled off together three hours ago. *Oh great. Let the manhunt begin.*

After searching in vain for the longest thirty minutes ever, I started to panic. What would I tell his mother? *Remember that time when you lost your engagement ring and I was so calm, understanding, and nonviolent? Well. . . .*

I'm sure most parents reading this story can relate to misplacing a child once or twice. Fortunately, I found William before I had to tell his mother that I had lost him. He had taken a wrong trail, gotten lost, and eventually found his way back. Facing Deborah would have been the scariest moment of my life — maybe the final moment of my life. *What are you so upset about? We have two more, and we can always have another one.*

Losing Jesus in the Midst of Religion

Losing an engagement ring is not good. Losing a son is bad. But losing Jesus is absolutely the worst. Luke records the strange story of Joseph and Mary losing Jesus — while doing their religious duty. Reading that story in the Bible made me feel better after losing my son.

> Every year his parents went to Jerusalem for the Feast of the Passover. When he was twelve years old, they went up to the Feast, according to the custom. After the Feast was over, while his parents were returning home, the boy Jesus *stayed behind* in Jerusalem, but *they were not aware* of it. Thinking he was in their company, they traveled on for a day. (Luke 2:41–44)

All who want to live Christ-centered lives could learn a lesson or two from this story.

First of all, notice that they lost Jesus while doing their religious duty. Sadly, it's common for Christian people and Christian organizations to lose Jesus while doing His work. So many mission and relief organizations started out Christ-centered, and while they continue to do good work, they no longer include Him or His message. Europe is littered with old, empty church buildings that should remind us that even churches often lose Jesus.

Secondly, they lost Jesus, but didn't realize it. I once left my cell phone in a New York City cab and didn't realize it until I was at the gate about to board my flight, and I reached into my pocket to call Deborah. The next four days were so peaceful that I often wonder why I replaced that phone. Many people and ministry programs are no longer Christ-centered, and they don't even realize it. Unlike my lost phone, losing Jesus does not produce peace.

Thirdly, they assumed Jesus was with them, but He was not. Mary and Joseph had traveled a full day, thinking Jesus was still with them. They just assumed, but their assumption was wrong. When churches and ministries lose Jesus as the center, it usually happens because we just assume He will always be with us. That type of religious presumption happens all the time in churches and ministries.

The Wrong Center

I don't know why, but it is easy for a church to start out Christ-centered, only to end up replacing Jesus with something else at the center. Here are some common centers that replace Jesus in well-meaning churches and ministries.

- **The preacher-centered church.** Everything revolves around the great man of God, the Christian celebrity who acts like the second coming of Abraham, Moses, Elijah, and Paul all wrapped into one lean, mean ministry machine. If he leads a mega-church, this guy always has his own TV show, and probably a jet or two. If he leads a small church, he has his own parking space and a small but dedicated gaggle of devoted fans.

- **The experience-centered church.** This is the place where everything is centered around hair-raising, spine-tingling, religious experiences that are impossible to explain. There is nothing wrong with powerful, inexplicable religious experiences, until we start following signs and wonders rather than following Jesus. Sadly, that is exactly what often happens.

- **The worship-centered church.** Worship is important, but the worship of worship is sickening. And, it's common. When our experience of "The Presence" becomes more important than the Person who is present, we have the wrong center. Often the worship-centered church is all about us, the people, while the Christ-centered church is all about the Person who is present, Jesus. There's a big difference.

- **The doctrine-centered church.** Correct doctrine is essential, but it should never replace the Person of Christ at the center. Those obsessed with pet doctrines feel they are the Guardians of the Ring, the Keepers of the Flame. Usually few outside their group really care about their particular nuanced doctrinal perspective, but they think nothing is more important. These churches tend to spread by division rather than multiplication. I recently heard this technique referred to as "church-splanting," which I learned is a combination of church-planting and church-splitting.

- **The cause-centered church.** Yes, a church should have a compassionate cause, a compelling vision, and a global mission. But the cause, no matter how important, should never be the center. Jesus is the ultimate cause. He is the mission. He is the *visio beatifica*, the Beautiful Vision. Make sure He remains the center of your vision and all your events.

- **The meeting-centered church.** The church meets on Sunday (or whenever), but the church is not the Sunday meeting. I hate boring meetings and I love excellence, but sometimes, in our desire to create compelling worship environments, the meeting can replace Jesus as the center of our attention. Our services are important, but the ultimate goal of meeting together is meeting Jesus.

- **The fellowship-centered church.** The New Testament is full of "one another" exhortations. We're supposed to love each other, and we're supposed to be a spiritual family and a caring community. But our relationships with one another should never replace Jesus at the center, though they often do.

The Born Supremacy

I've tried to illustrate what church might look like when something replaces Jesus at the center. Paul uses two words in his letter to the Colossians that I think aptly describe the Christ-centered church. He writes, "He is the head of the body, the church; he is the beginning and the firstborn from among the dead, so that in *everything* he might have the *supremacy*" (Colossians 1:18).

The first key word is "everything." Jesus is supposed to be the center of everything—not just religious and eternal things. Everything certainly includes Sunday, but also Monday through Saturday. Jesus should be the center of every sermon and every song, every prayer meeting and every worship service, every individual and every family. Everything.

The second word is "supremacy." Jesus is not to be the top priority on our long list of priorities, the first of many. Rather, He is to have supremacy, meaning He is the foundation and the cornerstone, the starting line and the finish line. He is the beginning, the middle, and the end. He is the ultimate. Nothing compares. Nothing competes.

Supremacy in everything!

The Hundred-Year Question

In his devotional classic, *No Man Is an Island*, Thomas Merton describes the hell of living self-centered rather than Christ-centered lives: "To consider persons and events and situations only in the light of their effect on myself is to live on the doorstep of hell. . . . Truth never becomes clear *as long as we assume that each of us, individually, is the center of the universe.*"

Another smart dead guy, DeVern Fromke, describes the "God-centered" life in his book, *No Other Foundation*:

> Everything should be adjusted and related to God for His purpose, pleasure, and satisfaction. Instead of man living in his own viewpoint where he interprets and relates all things to himself, it is God who lifts man up into His ultimate viewpoint where he can appreciate the glory, wisdom, and design of *a God-centered universe.*

What will happen to Every Nation in the next one hundred years if we lose Jesus as our center? What will Every Nation look like in one hundred years if we keep Jesus at the center of everything we do, say, pray, and preach?

FIVE

THE WEIRD AND THE DEAD

I remind you that there are churches so completely out of the hands of God that if the Holy Spirit withdrew from them, they wouldn't find it out for many months.
— A.W. Tozer

You will receive power when the Holy Spirit comes on you; and you will be my witnesses in Jerusalem, and in all Judea and Samaria, and to the ends of the earth.
— Jesus (Acts 1:8)

GOD HAS CALLED Every Nation Churches & Ministries *to honor God by establishing Christ-centered, Spirit-empowered, socially responsible churches and campus ministries in every nation.* But what does "Spirit-empowered" mean?

My friend and colleague Kevin York describes two ditches that churches often fall into when they lose their balance and run off the road. Kevin calls the ditch on the left "weird" and the ditch on the right "dead." Some churches are so experience-driven in the quest to become "spirit-filled" that they become weird. Others are so devoid of the Spirit that they are dead. Being truly Spirit-filled and Spirit-empowered will keep us out of both ditches.

In order to avoid both ditches, it might be a good idea for us to listen to the wise counsel of George Mueller (1805–1898), who knew a thing or two about the power and presence of the Holy Spirit. In his book, *Answers to Prayer,* Mueller reveals the key to avoiding the weird and the dead. He writes, "The Spirit and the Word must be combined. If I look to the Spirit alone without the Word, I lay myself open to great delusions. Also, if the Holy Ghost guides us at all, He will do it according to the Scriptures and never contrary to them." I'm grateful that my spiritual journey included a strong foundation of the Word and the Spirit.

My Encounter with the Holy Spirit

Ron Musselman, freshly graduated from Reformed Theological Seminary (RTS), was serious about his new job as the youth pastor of First Presbyterian Church in Jackson, Mississippi. So serious, that he constantly visited my high school, sharing the Gospel with every student who wanted to listen, and with some who didn't. I was definitely in the group that didn't. But that didn't deter Ron. Eventually, I surrendered to Christ. Then, discipleship started in earnest.

Several times our little discipleship group met on the RTS campus. After Bible study and prayer, Ron would take us to the campus bookstore and encourage us to purchase thick, heavy, expensive theological books. I bought some of the recommended books, and though I didn't comprehend much, I attempted to read them.

The key words in the above paragraphs are "Reformed" and "Presbyterian."

About a year after responding to the Gospel and faithfully attending Ron's weekly discipleship group, my big brother returned home from college for a weekend visit and took me with him to a church that was more Charismatic-Pentecostal than Reformed-Presbyterian. The people were friendly, the preaching was biblical, but the worship was like nothing I had ever experienced at First Presbyterian. The singing went on and on and on, and no one seemed to care. Eyes closed, hands raised, tears flowed — these people were so focused on Jesus that no one really noticed anything or anyone. I was probably the only person looking around the room and was surprised to see a few African-Americans and Latinos sprinkled in with the snow-white crowd. Ethnic diversity in worship was a sign and a wonder in Jackson, Mississippi, in 1976.

The key words in the previous paragraph are "Charismatic" and "Pentecostal."

In a few months, after hundreds of questions, dozens of books, hours of personal study, and much prayer, I was baptized in the Holy Spirit during a worship service on a Sunday night. No one prayed for me. No one laid hands on me. During a moment of intense worship, as the whole congregation began to "sing in the Spirit," I experienced an infilling of the Holy Spirit, and I joined hundreds of others singing in a heavenly language. For the next few months, I had an insatiable hunger for God's Word, and it seemed to jump off the page as I read. It was like I became addicted to Bible reading and Bible study. The way I experienced this baptism in the Holy Spirit seemed to line up with stories in the Book of Acts. As I read church history, I discovered that many of my spiritual heroes often wrote about their encounters with the Holy Spirit.

Please note that I am not implying that my Reformed-Presbyterian experience was dead or that my Charismatic-Pentecostal experience was weird. Far from it. I'm thankful that most of my spiritual history avoided both ditches. I have been asked if I am a Presbyterian, and I have been asked if I am a Pentecostal. If anything, I guess I'm a "Presbycostal," embracing both the Presbyterian and Pentecostal parts of my heritage.

A Spirit-Empowered Ministry

D.L. Moody (1837–1899) was perhaps the most effective evangelist of the nineteenth century. His impact was felt on both sides of the Atlantic. Most importantly, he committed much of his effort to equipping and empowering thousands of college students to serve as missionaries on their campuses and around the world.

After Moody's death, Evangelist R.A. Torrey (1856–1928) was asked to give a series of lectures on the topic "Why God Used D.L. Moody." Those lectures were published under the same title in 1923. According to Torrey, "The secret of why God used D. L. Moody was that he had a very definite enduement with power from on high, a very clear and

definite baptism with the Holy Ghost." Here's how Moody described
his Holy Spirit experience:

> I began to cry as never before, for a greater blessing from God.
> The hunger increased; I really felt that I did not want to live any
> longer. I kept on crying all the time that God would fill me with
> His Spirit. Well, one day in the City of New York — Oh! What
> a day, I cannot describe it; I seldom refer to it. It is almost too
> sacred an experience to name. Paul had an experience of which
> he never spoke for fourteen years. I can only say, God revealed
> Himself to me, and I had such an experience of His love that I
> had to ask Him to stay His hand.

What is both inspirational and instructional for us is how consistently Moody asked the younger Torrey to preach and teach on the
baptism with the Holy Spirit. Torrey said that he couldn't count the
number of times. Once, when Torrey had been invited to preach in the
prestigious Fifth Avenue Presbyterian Church in New York, Moody
showed up at his house just before Torrey was leaving:

> "Torrey, I just want to ask one thing of you," he began. "I want
> you to preach that sermon of yours on the baptism with the
> Holy Ghost." Time and time again Moody would arrange for
> Torrey to speak in a church and would request the same ser-
> mon. Finally, Torrey asked, "Mr. Moody, don't you think I have
> any sermons?" "Never mind that," Moody replied, "You give
> them that sermon; that's what they need to hear."

During the 1894 Northfield Students' Conference in Massachusetts — a gathering of university students not unlike Every Nation's
Campus Harvest and Ignite conferences — Moody repeated his standard request of Torrey to preach about the Holy Spirit. Saturday night's
sermon was about the baptism in the Holy Spirit — "what it is, what it
does, the need of it, and the possibility of it." Torrey's Sunday morning
sermon was also about the baptism in the Holy Spirit — and this time
on "how to get it."

When that service ended, Moody invited the students to gather for
prayer at 3:00 p.m. but added, "Some of you cannot wait for three hours.

Go to your rooms, go out into the woods, go to your tent, go anywhere where you can get alone with God and have this matter out with Him."

The students gathered at 3:00 as Moody had instructed. After many testimonies, Moody said, "I can't see any reason why we shouldn't kneel down here right now and ask God that the Holy Ghost may fall upon us just as definitely as He fell upon the apostles on the Day of Pentecost. Let us pray."

Torrey wrote about this moment: "As we began to pray, our prayers seemed to pierce that cloud and the Holy Ghost fell upon us. Men and Women, that is what we all need — the Baptism with the Holy Ghost."

Just as the Holy Spirit empowered the original disciples to become witnesses in Jerusalem, Judea, Samaria, and the ends of the world, the outpouring of the Holy Spirit in this conference would birth the Student Volunteer Movement for Foreign Missions. In the next decade, over five thousand American students would volunteer through this movement to serve as cross-cultural missionaries all over the world.

Consulting and the Holy Spirit

My friend, Ed Stetzer, is an author, speaker, and researcher who serves as a consultant to a number of denominations and mission groups, including Every Nation. Ed's client list includes some of the largest and oldest Charismatic and Pentecostal denominations in the world. After a consultation with a group of Pentecostal denominational leaders in 2010, Ed's assessment was that they had gradually lost their Charismatic-Pentecostal distinctive, and that if they didn't re-emphasize the baptism in the Holy Spirit and spiritual gifts, especially speaking in tongues, their decline would continue.

That was surprising advice coming from a man with masters' and doctoral degrees from Southern Baptist educational institutions. Speaking in tongues is not a part of Ed's Baptist church practice or theological position. Yet, Ed understands the danger of losing what, in a half-century, turned a small group of Pentecostals into a global movement and a distinct denomination. When Ed told that story to Kevin and me, the point he was making is that Every Nation better hold on to our foundational core distinctives and doctrines.

Distinctives attract some people. They repel others. Some people will love the way we do ministry. Others will hate it. Both attracting and repelling are good for a movement and for a local church. No matter the response, we must hold to what matters and to what made us who we are.

Missional or Mystical?

I've attended almost every kind of worship service in every cultural setting imaginable. One thing I've learned over the years and through those many experiences, is that we cannot judge what is or is not Spirit-empowered by our own cultural background. Periodically, we have to address this issue when Every Nation members go on mission trips and experience worship services in other nations. It's common for some to come home with the feeling that there is no moving of the Spirit in their home church's worship because it doesn't look or feel like their recent worship experience on the mission field.

I've participated in a Spirit-empowered worship service at St. Aldates, a liturgical Anglican Church in a medieval building. I have also experienced a Spirit-empowered worship service at Realms of Glory Church in Lagos, Nigeria, that was extremely different from my Oxford Anglican experience. And I have had the privilege of enjoying Spirit-empowered worship while sitting silently on the floor with underground Chinese house-church leaders, hoping we wouldn't be raided by the police. If people aren't falling down and shouting in tongues, it doesn't mean the power of the Holy Spirit isn't present. But it's also important to note that volume and emotion aren't always evidence of a move of the Holy Spirit either. Whether a worship experience is quiet, contemplative, and carefully planned, or loud, exuberant, and free-flowing, God can be honored, Christ can be at the center, and the Holy Spirit can come in power.

When asked what I think about the evidence of the baptism with the Holy Spirit, I usually quote from the book of Acts, which says, "But you will receive power when the Holy Spirit comes on you; and you will be my *witnesses* in Jerusalem, and in all Judea and Samaria, and to the ends of the earth" (Acts 1:8).

According to this passage, the evidence of being Spirit-empowered is that we become witnesses for Christ. In other words, we become more missional, not more mystical. When we confine the power of the Holy Spirit to our private life or to a worship service, we're missing the point. The result of being Spirit-empowered is that the apostles became bold, public witnesses to the resurrection and to the Gospel. It's understandable that everyone has a different style and approach to his or her witness. The foremost evidence of being filled and baptized with the power of the Holy Spirit is that we are bearing fruit. That's how we "prove to be His disciples" (John 15:8).

The book of Acts includes five accounts of people initially being filled with the Holy Spirit. The following table summarizes the method, manifestation, and results. Notice that three of the five accounts happened through the laying on of hands. Three of the five mentioned speaking in tongues, plus Paul told the Corinthians that he spoke in tongues more than them all. That means four of five spoke in tongues. And in the Acts 8 account, Simon saw and presumably heard something that made him want to buy the power of the Holy Spirit. What did he see and hear? We're not sure, but my best guess would include speaking tongues along with other spiritual gifts. And finally, we see that the result of people being filled with the Holy Spirit usually included the spread of the Gospel.

Verse	Method	Manifestation	Result
Acts 2:1–6	God	Wind, tongues of fire, spoke in tongues	Gospel preached in multiple languages
Acts 8:14–20	Praying and laying on of hands	Simon saw something	Simon desires the Holy Spirit; apostles reject money
Acts 9:17–20	Laying on of hands	Scales fell from eyes, spoke in tongues	Gospel preached by Paul
Acts 10:44–46	Sermon	Spoke in tongues	Gentiles receive Holy Spirit
Acts 19:1–6	Laying on of hands	Spoke in tongues, prophesied	Gospel preached in all of Asia

Filling and Refilling

In the early days of the church, the disciples were hiding behind closed doors in fear. Then, after the outpouring of the Holy Spirit, they were suddenly speaking boldly in the name of Jesus, addressing the same crowd who had recently shouted, "Crucify Him! Crucify Him!"

Soon enough, Spirit-inspired boldness was on display again. Peter and John were arrested for preaching the Gospel and healing the sick. Now, standing in chains in front of the religious leaders, boldness took over. Luke records what happened next:

> Then Peter, *filled with the Holy Spirit*, said to them, "Rulers and elders of the people, if we are on trial today for a benefit done to a sick man, as to how this man has been made well, let it be known to all of you and to all the people of Israel, that by the name of Jesus Christ the Nazarene, whom you crucified, whom God raised from the dead — by this name this man stands here before you in good health." (Acts 4:8–10)

The New American Standard Bible footnotes the literal translation of the Greek as "having just been filled." I doubt that what Peter and John said to the scribes and Pharisees was completely new. It was probably the same thing they had been proclaiming to the crowds — their testimony of Christ's resurrection. But it is pretty clear that *having just been filled* with the Spirit affected how they said it. The Jewish leaders were astonished at the courage and boldness with which Peter and John spoke.

On two other occasions, the apostles were said to have been filled with the Spirit yet again — Peter and John after they were threatened by the Pharisees (Acts 4:29–31), and Paul and Barnabas when they were opposed by the sorcerer Elymas (Acts 13:9–12). In both instances, having just been filled with the Holy Spirit, they responded to the challenges with extraordinary power and boldness.

One-and-Done Encounters with the Holy Spirit

People commonly make two mistakes about the Holy Spirit. Some arm themselves with theological arguments about how they got everything they needed when they were saved, and, consequently, have no need for an initial baptism or filling with the Spirit. The other mistake is to assume that an initial baptism of the Holy Spirit is a one-and-done experience. When asked if they are filled with the Spirit, they might respond, "Absolutely, I was filled with the Holy Spirit at a Victory Weekend in 2001!" Being filled with the Holy Spirit is not a merit badge to obtain, sew on your shirt, and wear for the rest of your life. Although in Scripture, the baptism of the Holy Spirit is typically a post-salvation experience, the apostles seemed to also consider being filled with the Spirit as a recurring experience. The accounts in Acts show that they were filled with the Holy Spirit *again*, and they went out speaking boldly *again*.

How do we get so filled with His Spirit that we live as bold witnesses for Christ? Paul answers that question by contrasting the Holy Spirit's infilling with getting drunk. "Do not get drunk with wine, which leads to debauchery. Instead, be filled with the Spirit" (Ephesians 5:18). I love John Piper's comment on this verse from his book, *A Godward Life, Book Two*:

> How do you get drunk with wine? Drink it! Lots of it. So how then shall we get drunk (filled) with the Spirit? Drink it! Lots of it. Paul said in 1 Corinthians 12:13, "We were all made to drink of one Spirit." Jesus said, "If anyone thirsts, let him come to me and drink. He who believes in me, as the scripture has said, 'Out of his heart shall flow rivers of living water.' Now this he said about the Spirit."

The Holy Spirit and the Great Commission
In Luke's account of the Great Commission, Jesus stressed to His disciples the necessity of being endued with power from on high *before* attempting to preach the Gospel to the nations:

> Repentance and forgiveness of sins should be proclaimed in his name to all nations, beginning from Jerusalem. You are witnesses of these things. And behold, I am sending the promise of my Father upon you. *But stay in the city until you are clothed with power from on high.* (Luke 24:47–49 ESV)

In the book of Acts, Luke tells what happened when they waited for the power (Acts 2), and then, story by story, he shows how the disciples continually relied on the Holy Spirit in preaching the Good News. Stephen, the first Christian martyr, was *full of the Holy Spirit* as he spoke the Word of God to the Sanhedrin (Acts 7:54–56). Philip the evangelist heard the Spirit tell him to engage the Ethiopian official seated on a chariot while he was reading the book of Isaiah (Acts 8:27–35). The Holy Spirit spoke to Peter to set aside his prejudice toward the Gentiles so he could minister to Cornelius and his household (Acts 10:19–48). While the leaders of the church at Antioch were worshiping the Lord and fasting, the Holy Spirit spoke to them to send Barnabas and Saul as missionary church planters (Acts 13:1–3).

The Hundred-Year Question

When I look to the future of Every Nation Churches & Ministries, I'm not so concerned about the form of our worship services and prayer meetings. What really concerns me is that we experience the power of the Holy Spirit, teach the baptism in the Holy Spirit, and practice the gifts and fruit of the Spirit in our daily lives. In other words, what matters is that we receive power to be His witnesses on every campus, in every neighborhood, and in every nation.

Pastor Jim Laffoon voiced his concern about this topic to me in an e-mail message:

> We live in an hour when Third Wave pneumatology has deeply influenced the Charismatic-Pentecostal movement. Many "spirit-filled" churches no longer preach the Baptism of the Spirit as an experience that is typically separate and subsequent from salvation. I believe that when the Baptism of the Spirit ceases to be taught this way, people will end up with no Holy Spirit experience at all.

What will Every Nation become in one hundred years if we fail to pass the baton of the Holy Spirit and spiritual gifts to the next generation?

What will happen in Every Nation churches and campus ministries in the next one hundred years if we follow Moody's example and insist on teaching the Baptism in the Holy Spirit?

SIX

THE QUARTET
OF THE VULNERABLES

If you can't feed a hundred people, then feed just one.
— Mother Teresa

Whatever you did for one of the least of these brothers
and sisters of mine, you did for me. Whatever you did
not do for the least of these, you did not do for me.
— Jesus (Matthew 25:40)

EVERY NATION Churches & Ministries *exist to honor God by establishing Christ-centered, Spirit-empowered, socially responsible churches and campus ministries in every nation.* So, what should a "socially responsible" church or campus ministry look like?

First of all, how we attempt to honor God "in every nation" should be unique to every culture and community because the needs and opportunities in each are different. What every expression of social responsibility should have in common is that it is unapologetically Christ-centered.

Slumdog Non-Millionaires
My friends Kevin and Lynette Menezes are living examples of what social responsibility looks like in Mumbai, India. The Every Nation work in Mumbai began in 2005, with the arrival of the Menezes and their three children. While the primary focus of the new church was

campus ministry and discipleship training, soon God opened two unique doors to serve the poor.

Responding to an invitation from Catholic nuns who run a shelter housing young girls from abusive backgrounds, Lynette Menezes, with a small team of college girls, began making regular visits to help these girls with their studies and to teach them about personal hygiene. In time, they began to share the Gospel with these girls who had been abandoned by their parents.

The second open door was another unexpected cry for help. (Have you noticed that God's calling often comes in the form of people crying for help?) Again, it was an opportunity to aid helpless children. Doris, a relative of Pastor Kevin, conducted a summer program for children born to prostitutes in Mumbai's brothels. Hearing that Every Nation Mumbai had a bunch of energetic university students, Doris asked Kevin if he would recruit a group of students to handle a day-long program for about fifty kids.

Kevin and the Every Nation students, some from high-caste Hindu families, had no idea what to expect. Their objective was to serve one day and be done with it. If things went well, maybe they would come back for a day or two the next summer. But meeting these children from the brothels had a life-changing impact on Kevin and the students. It broke their hearts and changed their church.

Kevin was clear about his calling to reach college students — the future leaders of the nation. As opportunities like this one presented themselves, he thought he would set aside a day or two as "reasonable Christian service." However, God had a bigger plan for Kevin and the whole Mumbai church.

What initially seemed like an invitation to help out for a day, eventually led to the launch of the "Transformers Club," the social service and development arm of Every Nation Mumbai. Since its launch in 2008, Transformers Club has been reaching into the darkest areas of Mumbai by serving children living in brothels and ministering to sex workers and mothers who are in bondage to prostitution. They also have a growing work with some of Mumbai's one million street children.

Here's Pastor Kevin's summary of how and why his church is intentional about social responsibility:

> Our church consists of about fifty students and has minimal resources. It would have been so easy to avoid the decision to begin a work with the poor and needy. However, I could sense the Holy Spirit in my heart, and I knew God wanted us to act and not delay. Every day we are faced with the realities of life in our city, and like many, we could have chosen to turn a blind eye. However, we made a decision to make a difference. Every life changed is a generation changed.

Being Socially Responsible in Every Nation

And that's not the only story. There are similar ones in almost every city where an Every Nation church is established.

Discovering that over half the children in Child Protective Services in Midland and Odessa, Texas, were sent out of the region because there weren't enough foster homes available, Pastor Dan and Kayla Stephens organized twenty area churches and transformed the foster care system in their community. In the last two years, the movement called One More Home has added over two hundred local families to the foster care system. Daniel and Kayla have served as foster parents to three kids and are currently working on a possible adoption.

In order to help underprivileged Filipino students stay in school, Dr. Joey Castro, pastor of Victory-Pasig, started paying for their lunch and transportation expenses out of his pocket. Soon, other church members joined Doc Joey in his effort to keep kids in school and off the streets. Eventually, this expression of generosity became the Real Life Foundation. Since 2007, Real Life has awarded over eight hundred scholarships and now operates twenty-five Real Life Centers across the Philippines. In almost every case, these Real Life scholars are the first in their family to earn a university degree.

Masiphane Projects serve abandoned and orphaned babies of HIV-positive parents, as well as young children from extreme poverty. Through Baby Haven, Child Haven, and other homes, Masiphane

Projects compassionately minister the love of Jesus to the most needy and neglected people in the Johannesburg, South Africa, metro area.

I'm writing this chapter in Nashville. Where I'm working, I can hear my friend, Greg Wark, talking on the phone, arranging finances to care for another recently rescued child-trafficking victim. This precious little girl is one of hundreds who have been saved through their efforts. Security protocols forbid me from giving details, but that scared little girl is thankful.

As Every Nation churches and campus ministries continue to multiply and spread around the world, so do our compassion ministries. However, no one in our churches is waiting for the Every Nation national or regional office to solve the world's problems. Almost all these efforts and organizations are the initiative of an Every Nation local church and of local church members. Lives are changed because hundreds of churches and thousands of people make the decision to daily stand in the gap for people in great need. Relief and development teams, short-term medical missions, inner-city after-school programs, adoption services, and many similar initiatives are springing up in every city where an Every Nation local church is established — so much so, it is impossible to track it all.

Who Are Your People?

In the Deep South where I grew up (Mississippi), people feel the need to get a fix on who you are and where you came from. If you don't look familiar, and people don't immediately recognize your name, the next question is probably going to be, "Who are your people?" In that context, the question refers to your parents and grandparents. That's how Southerners identify and categorize you. Working their way back to some recognizable ancestor, they'll declare with a sigh of satisfaction and a slap on the back, "Oh yeah, I know who you are!" In the same way, a lot of people today are trying to get a fix on God, trying to figure out what He is like, and who His people are.

What separates God in Scripture from all other religious ideas about God is that He personally identifies Himself with the lowest classes. He became one of them. Remember, He introduced His Son to the world as a blue-collar construction worker who was born in a barn. Scripture consistently reveals the Father as someone who identified with the needs of the most vulnerable. "These are My people," He seems to say.

Nicholas Wolterstorff, in his book, *Justice: Rights and Wrongs*, categorized those people of His as the "quartet of the vulnerables," the poor, the orphans, the sick, and the immigrants. He writes:

> [It's] because the orientation of Israel's writers was practical, rather than theoretical, that the *quartet of the vulnerable* low ones looms so large in their writings. What they say about justice and injustice occurs within the context of an imperative they had heard from Yahweh and that they now announced to their fellows: seek justice, undo the bonds of injustice. Israel's religion was a religion of salvation, not of contemplation — that is what accounts for the mantra of the widows, the orphans, the aliens, and the poor.

The Bible says it this way:

> For the LORD your God is the God of gods and the Lord of lords, the great, the mighty, and the awesome God who does not show partiality nor take a bribe. He executes justice for the orphan and the widow, and shows His love for the alien by giving him food and clothing. So show your love for the alien, for you were aliens in the land of Egypt. (Deuteronomy 10:17–18)

Not only does God identify Himself with the most vulnerable and disenfranchised people, He is very sensitive to anyone who messes with them — those who oppress them, those who take advantage of them, those who do them injustice, or those who simply ignore them. The

> **God**
> …of Abraham, Isaac, and Jacob,
> Father to the Fatherless,
> Defender of Widows,
> Helper of the Poor,
> Friend to the Foreigner,
> Champion of the Defenseless,
> Since the Creation of the World.

weaker and more defenseless the person, the more likely He is to assume the role of protector, defender, and champion of their cause. In fact, if God had a business card, it would look something like the one shown on the previous page.

These are the people with whom the Father identified over and over. He has declared it in no uncertain terms, "These are My people."

Like Father, Like Son

Jesus had a moral compass that guided and governed His words and actions. He explained it in a short sentence: "Very truly I tell you, the Son can do nothing by Himself; He can do only what He sees his Father doing, because whatever the Father does the Son also does" (John 5:19). In other words, when Jesus arrived on earth as the incarnate Son of God, He simply got busy doing the same things He had seen the Father doing. And what did the Son of God do? He preached the Gospel to the poor, including children and widows, helped a lot of sick people (Matthew 11:4–6), and reached out to foreigners (the Romans and Samaritans). He condemned those who oppressed the needy, as well as those who simply did nothing to help (the rich man and Lazarus; the good Samaritan). He pronounced woes upon the Pharisees who were big on religion but not all that concerned about needy people. In all of these situations, Jesus was showing us what the Father was really like by identifying with those in need and becoming their advocate.

Historically, the church has gone from ditch to ditch on this issue. It is strangely common for God-fearing individuals and Christian organizations to wander farther and farther away from the Gospel as they go about serving the needs of the poor and oppressed. Offering only temporal relief for physical needs, they find themselves stuck in one ditch without the power of the Gospel to get out.

On the other hand, some evangelicals love to preach the Gospel while ignoring the temporal-but-real needs of the hungry, marginalized, and oppressed. More often than not, this form of "reaching out without reaching down" is done by selective evangelism — surrounding ourselves and our churches with people very much like us, people who are unlikely to be one of those vulnerables. We see this same strategy in the Parable of the Good Samaritan when two pious religious leaders walked on the other side of the road (into the opposite ditch) in order to avoid a man who needed their help.

Why does it have to be either/or? Why not both? Why not care for the poor and preach the Gospel, like Jesus did?

Vacation or Mission?

A couple of weeks ago, I had lunch with a friend who is a successful entrepreneur in Nashville. He wanted to ask me about mission opportunities, especially to the poor. This man takes his family on a five-star vacation every summer. But, unlike many financially successful Christians, he often adds a mission experience on the front end of the family holiday. A week of mission followed by a week of vacation — that's how his family rolls. One summer he took his wife and kids on a mission vacation to the Philippines. First, they ministered to squatter kids in Manila's slums, and then they were off to the beautiful white sand beaches of Boracay. Every year, his kids end up with as many unforgettable memories of the family mission to the poor as they do the family vacation with the rich and famous.

Last summer's mission trip included a week in India working with our Every Nation church there, spreading the love of Jesus to the children of Mumbai's sex workers. My friend proudly recounted that his pre-teen daughter told him that after she graduates in a few years, she wants to return to Mumbai to work with Kevin and Lynette and help those kids.

The Hundred-Year Question

We are called to establish "socially responsible" churches and campus ministries in every nation. What will Every Nation become in one hundred years if we ignore the poor and needy? What could happen in one hundred years if we continue to serve the poor and underprivileged in our cities?

SEVEN

THE ABCs

The Church is the hope of the world.

— Bill Hybels

I will build my church and the gates of Hades will not overcome it.

— Jesus (Matthew 16:18)

IF WE EXIST *to honor God by establishing Christ-centered, Spirit-empowered, socially responsible churches and campus ministries in every nation*, then we need to talk about the Church and church planting.

I have noticed a strange and disturbing trend recently. It seems that the really cool Christians are somewhat anti-church. And strangely enough, even the cool *churches* are anti-church. It has become hip to love Jesus, but hate the Church. I know this makes no sense, but when being cool is the ultimate issue, I guess it doesn't have to make sense. This is primarily a Western church problem, but with the proliferation of blogs, podcasts, and tweets, unfortunately, it will probably spread.

Admitting what I really feel about the local church is about as cool as a man my age wearing skinny jeans, but here I go: I love Jesus and I love His Church. I can't help it. Here's why. I first heard the Gospel at a church youth camp. I got baptized in the Holy Spirit at a church worship service. I learned how to be a disciple through a church youth group. I met my wife at a church conference. I raised my sons in church. I met most of my life-long friends at church.

I agree with Pastor Bill Hybels who constantly says and writes, "The local church is the hope of the world." And I agree with the Bible when it says the Church is "the pillar and foundation of the truth" (1 Timothy 3:15). That "pillar and foundation of truth" statement seemed backwards to me at first. Isn't the truth the foundation of the Church? But Paul says the Church is the foundation of the truth. In other words, the Church upholds, undergirds, and validates the truth. This high view of the Church compels us to passionately plant new churches.

A Church-Planting Story

Twenty years ago, Ron Miller was presented with two career opportunities. The first option was to play professional basketball in Japan and work in a Japanese company in the off-season as a corporate fitness director. The total compensation package included over $250,000 a year, plus endorsement income and the opportunity to see the world. The second option was to stay in Tallahassee, Florida, where Ron had lived his whole life, and to work as an assistant strength coach for the Florida State University (FSU) Athletic Department, while helping plant a new church. The total salary package for the FSU coaching option? $9,000 a year. The compensation for helping with the new church? Zero.

After some serious prayer, Ron chose the Tallahassee option. Not a great career move in the eyes of some, but in Ron's words, "I figured Jesus was more into church planting than playing basketball." Ron accepted the job as the assistant strength coach and worked as a volunteer leader of Every Nation Campus Ministries' FSU chapter. His ministry work included mission trips to Africa and church-planting outreaches in Baltimore and Philadelphia in the homes of professional football players who had been members of Every Nation Tallahassee while in college at FSU.

Five years after establishing the Every Nation church in Tallahassee, Ron's pastor and childhood friend, Chip, relocated to Atlanta to start a new church. The entire worship team and most of the leaders moved to Atlanta to help the new church. About seventy students and a few families remained. Ron resigned from the FSU athletic staff to become the full-time pastor of this remnant.

As Ron and his wife, Cindy, immediately got busy making disciples, a whole new group of leaders began to emerge. Over the next eight years, Every Nation Tallahassee tripled in size, and helped plant, re-launch, or provide senior leaders for seven more churches — all while maintaining a strong local church presence in Tallahassee. That accomplishment was neither easy nor insignificant. Here's a quick summary of those years:

- The first to go was the associate pastor, Clay, who was an FSU football legend. He moved to Miami to do ministry.

- Then the next to leave was the youth pastor, Addison, who moved with his wife, Lisa, and their family to Europe to do mission work in Budapest and Edinburgh.

- Then Adam, the worship leader, moved to Scotland with his wife, Hope, to help start a new church. Adam took most of the worship team leaders with him. Again, Ron and Cindy were starting over, equipping and empowering new worship leaders.

- Then the next to leave was the campus pastor, Gabe, who went to Rutgers University to study mathematics. Ross took his place as campus pastor. After graduating from Rutgers with a PhD in mathematical physics, Gabe and his wife, Jennifer, became the lead pastors of the Every Nation church in Philadelphia, a church that Tallahassee people helped start in the late 1990s.

- Then the children's pastor, Clayton, planted a church in Tampa where he grew up. Of course, his wife, Kelly, who was the Tallahassee church's secretary, went with him.

- Then campus pastors Ross and Amy planted a new church in Miami. Donny and Janna replaced Ross and Amy on the campus.

- Adam and Hope decided to leave Scotland and plant a church to reach students in Boston, Massachusetts. FSU campus ministry leaders, Donnie and Janna, left Tallahassee to help Adam and Hope in Boston.

- And finally, in January 2013, preaching pastor, Adrian, and his wife, Wendy, launched a new Every Nation church in Tallahassee.

Though many of the these new churches are only a few years old, their combined attendance is almost three times the current size of Every Nation Tallahassee. Ron and Cindy Miller have lived their entire lives in Tallahassee, a sleepy college town in the Florida panhandle. They remain committed to campus ministry and church planting, and, most of all, to making disciples. They have a big vision that extends way beyond the city limits of Tallahassee.

Intentional church planting is not unique to Every Nation Tallahassee. I wish I had space and time to tell other church-planting stories, like Every Nation London planting churches in Poland, Belgium, China, Spain, and Ireland; and Every Nation Dubai planting churches in Abu Dhabi, Teheran, Mumbai, Sharjah, and Ras Al Khaimah; and Every Nation Auckland planting churches in Melbourne, Sydney, and Brisbane. The list goes on and on and on, but time does not.

I'm often asked how we're able to plant churches that plant other churches. That answer is as simple as ABCCC.

Do You Know Your ABCCCs?

Over the years, I've seen, studied, and/or tried to manage just about every approach to church planting known to man — all producing varying degrees of success. You've got the slow-growth model and the fast-growth model, the launch-big-or-go-home strategy, the old-school ready-fire-aim philosophy, the throw-money-at-it tactic, the massive-team concept, the organic house-church approach, the conspiracy-of-kindness movement, the big-bang theory, the missional mini-model, and so on. Many of these strategies contain valuable elements of establishing and growing new congregations. But none will guarantee church-planting success.

In the last twenty years, missiologists and church leaders have come a long way in demystifying the church-planting process and strategy. Today, unlike when I started as an accidental missionary, we are far less likely to simply attend a prayer meeting, feel a burden, buy a ticket, and go. (Not that this approach has not or will not be successful.) But often the people who use this "just go and trust God" strategy suffer unduly and grow slowly. Fortunately, we tend to be more intentional these days, evaluating that sense of calling and upgrading the level of preparation.

Every Nation's current church-planting strategy focuses on assessment, training, and continual support. The core elements of our process are Assessment Center, BootCamp, Coaching, Consulting, and Clusters — otherwise known as ABC3.

- **Assessment Center.** Every Nation's Assessment Center for Church Planters is open to any potential church planter who plans to launch a new church in the next twelve to eighteen months. It's designed to help candidates discern their calling and preparedness to lead a church-planting team by affirming strengths and identifying weaknesses.

- **BootCamp.** The objective of the Church-Planting BootCamp is to give church planters strategic and practical skills that will help break through current statistical norms by planting healthy, vibrant, growing churches that are committed to planting more churches that are healthy, vibrant, and growing. We've contextualized the principles and conducted these BootCamps in North America, Europe, Africa, Asia, and the Middle East. BootCamps last from one week to four months, depending on the region.

- **Coaching.** Our coaching network connects new church planters with veteran ministers and is designed to help during the first year of the new church. Coaching focuses these new pastors on their ongoing spiritual development, as well as their relational and leadership skills.

- **Consulting.** As churches are being established, Every Nation provides trained church consultants to help pastors grow healthy churches and develop strategies to effectively engage their cultures and impact their cities. Every Nation consultants specialize in helping new and established churches break through traditional growth barriers by focusing on church health and affirming core values, all while adjusting programs and priorities.

- **Clusters.** Clusters are regional gatherings of pastors and church
  planters with the aim of imparting vision, discussing best practices,
  and deepening relationships. In the Philippines, our clusters are
  called FUEL meetings (because they provide Focus, Unity, Equipping, and Leadership). In the Middle East, our cluster is the MESS
  (Middle East Strategic Summit). In Southern Africa, our cluster is
  the Mini-Daba. The phrase is a mixture of Zulu and English, the
  word *daba* being a short form of *indaba*, which means a gathering or meeting of chiefs. In Europe, our cluster meetings are done
  monthly via conference call, plus we have an annual face-to-face
  European Leaders Summit (ELS) to foster relational connection.
  It doesn't matter where we meet or what we call the meeting, every pastor and church planter needs relational connection and best
  practices, which is what clusters are all about.

Our ABC3 strategy seems to be working. According to the most
recent statistics from LifeWay Research, of fifty-four church-planting
movements in the United States, the average church has a membership or regular attendance of about eighty people after four years. The
typical size of an Every Nation church after four years is more than
double that figure. In the Philippines, the results are even more dramatic. Growth thresholds that previously took a decade to reach are
now happening in two to three years. Besides numerical growth, our
leaders are finding life-giving and life-saving relationships with peers
and mentors through our coaching, consulting, and cluster networks.
It's important to understand the four main reasons the ABC3 strategy
is working so effectively.

1. **Strong, healthy local churches.** Strong, healthy churches tend to
   plant strong, healthy churches. Large, growing churches tend to
   plant large, growing churches. Churches that make disciples tend
   to plant churches that make disciples. Churches that plant churches
   tend to plant churches that plant churches. Strong, healthy local
   churches are the starting point.

2. **Strong, healthy church planters.** The second reason our ABC3
   strategy is working is because of the quality of church-planting

candidates that are coming from strong, healthy local churches. If we have a great strategy, but a weak leader, the new church will be weak. If we have an abundance of capital and a great team, but a weak leader, the new church will fail. Our ABC3 strategy is working, not because it's the best strategy, but because we have some of the best church planters I have ever met.

3. **Strong, healthy campus ministries.** Most of our new church planters responded to the Gospel as university students. Many of them started out in ministry as campus missionaries. A season of campus ministry is the best possible work experience for a future church planter. The faith and diligence required to develop a partnership team, the communication and people skills required to work with students, and the spiritual disciplines required to lead any ministry are a great foundation for church-planting work.

4. **Strong, healthy discipleship.** My friend, David Houston, a veteran church planter who serves as one of our Every Nation North America church consultants, adds another key ingredient to the three above: discipleship. He says,

> Discipleship is the launching pad for new leaders. In our ABC3 assessment and training process for new church planters, we've realized that the best leaders come from churches that practice biblical discipleship. Because discipleship both equips and empowers leaders, it gives them the confidence necessary for successful church planting.

Intentionally Depleting the Leadership Ranks

As important as the process is, for a church-planting movement to continue multiplying, each individual pastor must be willing to release some of their best leaders. The best equipping in the world is ineffective until those we equip are also empowered — and often, empowering means sending.

I once attended a graduation ceremony of a leadership training school. Everyone was clapping and cheering and congratulating each other. Yet, no matter how much I tried, I had a difficult time celebrating, because I knew that there was no plan or strategy to empower the graduates to serve, minister, and lead. These students had learned basic theology and had developed rudimentary ministry skills, with no opportunity or platform to put any of it into practice. Church planting solves that problem. Sending church-planting teams creates space for multiple generations of ministers and leaders.

Leadership emerges when there's room to grow. Churches that are top heavy in leaders (especially paid-staff leadership) have a hard time empowering next-generation leaders. It doesn't matter how well we train and equip people, if no one leaves and creates leadership space, then there is no need, no opportunity, and no challenge to step forward.

Every Nation Tallahassee is a great example of this principle. With their commitment to campus ministry, combined with their commitment to sending out their best leaders to plant churches, Ron, Cindy, and their ever-diminishing team constantly create space for new leaders to emerge.

Kevin York, Every Nation's resident church-planting guru, says that churches that do not intentionally "deplete their leadership ranks by periodically planting new churches" will hit the wall and stagnate around the twenty-year mark. That explains why churches that don't reproduce tend to be dead, even if they're big.

The Hundred-Year Question

The calling of Every Nation is to establish churches and campus ministries in every nation. We're targeting cities all over the world that have a high concentration of university students. Currently, we have about two thousand Every Nation churches in sixty-five nations. That means there are 131 nations without an Every Nation church. Someone needs to go to those nations. How about you? Have you ever considered being a part of our church-planting initiative? Have you ever considered financially supporting our church-planting efforts worldwide? How about a commitment to pray for a particular nation or people-group? The Great Commission not only applies to all nations, but to all believers.

What will Every Nation become in one hundred years if we're not willing to equip, empower, and send leaders to establish new churches? What could happen in the next one hundred years if each Every Nation church would follow Every Nation Tallahassee's example and get serious about church planting?

EIGHT

THE FUTURE WORLD

> *Let every student be plainly instructed, and earnestly*
> *pressed to consider well, the main end of his life and*
> *studies is, to know God and Jesus Christ which is*
> *eternal life and therefore to lay Christ in the bottom,*
> *as the only foundation of all sound knowledge and*
> *learning.*
> — Harvard's "Rules and Precepts" (1646)
>
> *Remember your Creator in the days of your youth.*
> — Solomon (Ecclesiastes 12:1)

OUR MISSION is *to honor God by establishing Christ-centered, Spirit-empowered, socially responsible churches and campus ministries in every nation.* But why the campus?

A long, long time ago, Deborah and I were campus ministers, serving the students of Mississippi State University. And during our first few years in Manila, we were technically church planters, but since ninety percent of our church members were students, we felt more like campus missionaries than pastors. We loved ministering to students. Then time happened. I got old. And we became "real" pastors. But every now and then, I'm tempted to resign and become a campus missionary all over again.

Recently, that temptation was difficult to resist as I read this newspaper headline: "FAU Professor Tells Students to Stomp on Jesus." That FAU (Florida Atlantic University) professor, Dr. Deandre Poole, says he was simply following the textbook instructor's guide. Here's what the guide said:

> Have the students write the name JESUS in big letters on a piece of paper. Ask the students to stand up and put the paper on the floor in front of them with the name facing up. Ask the students to think about it for a moment. After a brief period of silence, instruct them to step on the paper.

After watching the news, I was deeply troubled that the name of Jesus would be used so flippantly in a college classroom. I wanted to get on a plane to South Florida and set up a *God Test* booth. But instead of signing up to be a campus missionary at FAU, Deborah and I flew to Manila. As soon as we landed, we got busy with church work, and now I'm sitting in Coffee Bean writing this chapter about the importance of campus ministry. As I write, I'm praying that thousands will surrender to the call and serve as missionaries to the great university campuses of the world.

I'm also praying that thousands will become professors. My oldest son William, a PhD student at Vanderbilt University, sent me a link to an article by an atheist that stated that the disrespect for Christians at FAU has gone too far. It's pretty bad when an atheist defends Jesus on campus. I responded to William's e-mail with this simple message, "The university campuses of the world need professors like you."

Campus Ministry in Southern Africa

Fortunately, it's not all bad news on the campus. Here's a good story: Roshni Meelun arrived at the University of Cape Town (UCT) in 2000 as a committed Hindu from Mauritius. For the geographically challenged among us, the Republic of Mauritius is an island nation in the Indian Ocean about two thousand kilometers (twelve hundred miles) off the southeast coast of Africa. Students from Every Nation befriended Roshni and engaged her with the Gospel. Eventually, she surrendered her life to Christ. After graduating top of her class from one of the premier universities in Africa, Roshni enrolled in the Every Nation School of Campus Ministry, where she trained for vocational ministry.

Today, she leads our Every Nation Campus Ministries' (ENCM) chapter at UCT.

Every week, 650 UCT students meet in 150 discipleship groups all over the campus, and over one thousand attend the Sunday worship service nearby. Full-time campus missionaries equip and empower students to serve as leaders in all spheres of campus life including student government, sports teams, and social clubs, as well as in student dormitories. Every year, ENCM students serve on the student government council. In fact, one year all twelve elected seats on the Student Representative Council were filled by ENCM students. This service isn't because of a "takeover" mentality, rather, it's the result of a servant's attitude the students have toward their campus.

And that's just one university.

The vision is to equip and empower students all over Southern Africa to engage their friends with the Gospel, to make disciples, and to develop leaders who will transform campus and culture. This vision is not just someone "dreaming the impossible dream." Under the leadership of Southern Africa ENCM directors Frans Olivier and Olajide Pariola, along with a team of dedicated campus missionaries, we're currently established on thirty-two campuses in Southern Africa. Our ENCM Southern Africa campus missionaries have equipped thousands of students with the *God Test*, an evangelism tool developed by Rice Broocks for engaging people in conversational evangelism. As a result, more than thirty-five hundred African students have surrendered to Christ in the last two years. The goal is to reach a "cultural tipping point" on every campus across the continent of Africa, resulting in cultural and national transformation.

Reaching a "Tipping Point" in Los Banos, Philippines
In 1989, Gilbert Foliente was a math major at the prestigious University of the Philippines, Los Banos (UPLB), and Ferdie Cabiling was a campus evangelist from Manila's University Belt. Their paths crossed one day in November when Ferdie was leading an outreach on the UPLB campus, about seventy-five kilometers south of Manila. Gilbert wandered into the meeting, heard the Gospel, and put his faith in

Jesus. Two years later, Gilbert, while still a student, became our campus ministry director at UPLB. As soon as he graduated in 1993, Gilbert became the lead pastor of Victory Los Banos and its thirty members.

During the second year of Gilbert's pastorate, American campus evangelist Steve Hollander visited the Philippines and radically impacted Gilbert and the Victory church in the rural college town of Los Banos. After two weeks of outreach meetings, which doubled the church from thirty to sixty, Steve challenged Gilbert: "When I come back in a year, you should have ten percent of the UPLB students in your church." Gilbert put that math degree to work: *UPLB has six thousand students, so Steve is expecting our church to grow from sixty to six hundred in twelve months. Really? Okay.*

Needless to say, they did not grow from sixty to six hundred in twelve months. But by the time Gilbert turned the UPLB church over to a recent UPLB grad, Jon Dolor, in 2005, the church had grown to twelve hundred, including over one thousand UPLB students. And, they had hit that cultural tipping point, impacting every area of the campus.

After passing the UPLB baton to Jon, Gilbert and Cathy moved from Los Banos to Manila to become the pastors of the original U-Belt church that Deborah and I planted in 1984. When they arrived, about nine hundred people attended the church, including three hundred students. Gilbert and Cathy got busy engaging, establishing, equipping, and empowering students. Now, every weekend, over seven thousand worship at Victory U-Belt. Over forty-five hundred of them are students. Not quite a tipping point in the middle of Manila's three-hundred thousand University Belt students, but it is a good start.

How One Church Lost and Reclaimed the Campus Vision
Every leader who's been involved in campus ministry knows that if reaching the campus becomes a side issue for a local church, suddenly, before we know it, all the students will graduate and our campus ministry will vanish. Pastor Seth Trimmer and his team provide a great example of an Every Nation church restarting a campus ministry after it had dwindled to almost nothing.

Seth responded to the Gospel through the Oregon State University ENCM chapter as an unchurched agnostic football player. After graduation, he joined a staff of seven full-time campus missionaries. Because of many ensuing difficulties in the church, by 2007, their campus ministry had "grown" from over *two hundred* to just *two*, and Seth was the lone remaining campus missionary. In July of that year, Seth became the lead pastor of the church, simply because he was the last man standing.

Seth recalls that, at that point, it didn't seem like they would ever have the momentum or resources to effectively reach the campus again. As he concentrated on leading the small church, he did his best to get their few students involved in church life. That was about all he could do with his limited budget and resources. As the congregation grew healthy and strong again, Seth made sure the church did not forget the campus. Here's how he explains their commitment:

> One of the membership sayings we have at Grace City Church is that you don't have to be actively on campus with students, but if you're a member of this church, then *you must care about students* and even be willing to defer personal preferences for their sake.

Eventually, something extraordinary began to happen. Students started trickling in. At first it was just a few; then they started pouring in. They weren't coming from campus meetings, but from the testimonies and invitations of their friends. Many of them didn't have a church background. They were just "exploring" Christianity. The students seem to be longing for spiritual family—brothers, sisters, mothers, fathers, and grandparents. And they found it as the rest of the church stepped up and connected with the students. Today, OSU has one of the largest and strongest ENCM chapters in North America.

Now, with a growing church filled with so many college students, Seth is often asked how many campus ministers he has working for him. His standard reply generally goes like this:

> Up until the past year—zero. But the truth is that we have at least a hundred campus ministers. They just aren't getting paid.

They are business people, soccer moms, grandparents, and empty nesters. They are people from all walks and stages of life who truly love the next generation and embrace the vision to reach the campus.

If you're attempting campus ministry in a tough community, here's the best part of the story. In the year Seth became the pastor (2007), Benton County, Oregon had the distinction of being the most unchurched county in the United States. Nonetheless, hundreds of students now stream out of OSU dorms, fraternity houses, and apartments every Sunday morning to walk to Grace City Church. According to Seth, the reasons are simple: "The major factors are a clear and compelling preaching of the Gospel, and the love the church community poured out family-style to all the students."

Eight Reasons We Must Reach the Campus

Throughout history, movements have published manifestos to encapsulate and communicate their mission. Most movements' manifestos have failed and been forgotten. Others, like the *Communist Manifesto,* and the *Humanist Manifesto,* have literally changed the world. Several decades ago, Rice Broocks penned the *Campus Manifesto,* stating the reasons we must reach the campus. Here's an updated version of Every Nation's *Campus Manifesto,* which has the potential to change the world:

1. **The future leaders of society are on our campuses.** It doesn't matter which nation we're talking about: their future leaders are on college and university campuses. Virtually all the world's presidents, prime ministers, senators, members of parliaments, bankers, lawyers, judges, teachers, doctors, and business leaders have passed through the college and university system. In other words, the campus is where we find the future influencers in every critical aspect of a nation's culture.

2. **Major movements, good and bad, start on the campus.** Whether it's spiritual revival or political revolution, the campus is the birthplace of change. Marxism, atheism, feminism, and practically every

other "ism" that has spread around the world, at one time, was a tiny seed on the university campus.

3. **The majority of people who become Christians do so as students.** Countless studies, both formal and informal, continue to confirm that most who surrender to Christ do so before their twenty-fifth birthday. How many of you reading this book responded to the Gospel before you were twenty-five?

4. **International students impact their nations.** International students represent the top one percent of students in their home nations. They're lining up at embassies around the world to secure visas to study in the UK, the USA, the UAE, Canada, South Africa, Australia, New Zealand, Singapore, the Philippines, and others. We frequently have children of business leaders, government officials, and even royalty in ENCM chapters around the world. Many of these international students come from nations that restrict or ban the Gospel. By reaching them while they're on our campuses, training them, and sending them home with the Gospel, we can revolutionize world missions. The USA alone hosts more than half a million international students. Will they return home with or without the Gospel after they graduate?

5. **The values on campus become the values in society.** The philosophy, morality, and ethics taught by professors on university campuses will, over the next decade, slowly but surely work their way into public policy, media, and education. As a result, those ideas and values are perpetuated through legislation, education, music, movies, literature, and media.

6. **The most available and trainable masses are on our campuses.** Students at universities are trying to figure out what to do with their lives. Since they have few obligations, they are unhindered when it comes to following Christ and answering the call to serve Him. The campus is not only the source of the next generation of business, government, and educational leaders, but it's also where we'll find the next generation of church leaders and cross-cultural missionaries.

7. **When we reach a student, we reach a family.** Often, moms and dads and brothers and sisters are impacted by the stories from students who return home with a changed life (or from students who have their grades raised from the dead after they meet Jesus). The New Testament pattern of church growth often included entire families turning to Christ. That's exactly what happened in my family. During a weekend visit home in his first year at college, my big brother invited me to church with him and started a spiritual chain reaction that impacted every member of our immediate family.

8. **God promised to pour out His Spirit upon sons and daughters.** (Acts 2:17). This scripture translates into an enormous awakening among the youth of the world, a coming global harvest of young people. We must be prepared to handle this harvest by sending campus missionaries to colleges and high schools, missionaries who are equipped and empowered to make disciples.

This list could go on forever, but these eight reasons should be enough to convince every leader and every church to prioritize reaching the campus.

Stewardship of a Unique Calling

The Holy Spirit sets apart individuals, ministries, and churches to reach specific people groups. God calls some people to reach street kids, some to reach prisoners, some to reach suburbanites, some to reach college students, and some to reach specific ethnic groups — just like Paul, the Apostle to the Gentiles, and Peter, the Apostle to the Jews.

> They recognized that I [Paul] had been entrusted with the task of preaching the gospel to the uncircumcised, just as Peter had been to the circumcised. For God, who was at work in Peter as an apostle to the circumcised, was also at work in me as an apostle to the Gentiles. (Galatians 2:7–8)

Paul not only saw himself as one who was called to a specific group, but also as one who would give an account to God for that mission.

> For if I preach the gospel, I have nothing to boast of, for I am under compulsion; for woe is me if I do not preach the gospel.

For if I do this voluntarily, I have a reward; but if against my will,
I have a stewardship entrusted to me. (1 Corinthians 9:16–17)

At this point, I need to clarify something. I'm not claiming that
Every Nation has been called and set apart with some kind of New
Testament apostolic calling like Paul. His calling was unique. After all,
he was one among many called to write part of the Bible. However, we
do feel a calling to the campus, and feel it so strongly that it defines
who we are. It's a calling that binds us together in a common cause.
Sometimes independent churches contact Every Nation looking for a
denomination to join. They're good people leading good churches, but
if they aren't willing to incorporate campus ministry into their mission, they need to keep looking. It's not that we don't like these people.
It's just that we have to be faithful to our calling, and so would anyone
who joins us.

Seth Trimmer understands our calling to the campus and leads his
church with a sense of stewardship. Here's his summary about church
and campus ministry in the Every Nation context:

I feel like Every Nation's great strength is the church-based campus ministry model. I think we have to fight the trend to define
church by Sunday events, potlucks, and board meetings — instead of a family of people on mission together. In Every Nation,
that means significantly, although not exclusively, that we reach
the campus.

A Million Ways to Reach the Campus

I wish I had time to tell you a hundred more stories about how Every
Nation churches are reaching students with the Gospel. Every story
in every city is unique. Seth and Grace City Church are reaching the
Oregon State University campus by empowering church members to
minister to students in small groups. Plus, Corvallis is a small college
town, and the church sits on the edge of OSU, making it convenient
for students to walk to church. Gilbert reached over ten percent of the
UPLB students in the rural campus town of Los Banos without any
full-time staff. He's now reaching thousands of students in Manila's

U-Belt with the help of seventeen well-trained campus missionaries. Olajide, Frans, Roshni, and the South Africans have 117 full-time staff and interns who are funded by teams of ministry partners. They're all based in local churches that are deeply committed to reaching the campus. Other Every Nation churches that are nowhere near a university campus are actively reaching out to the nearby high school campuses in order to reach the next generation.

The point is that there are a million ways to reach the campus. Different cultures and communities will require different strategies. Whether the church leadership team plants the church on the edge of campus or in multiple sites throughout the city, whether we used random church members as small group leaders or fully funded campus missionaries, some way, somehow, we must reach students with the Gospel. Woe to us if we don't.

The Hundred-Year Question

What will happen to Every Nation (and every nation) in the next one hundred years if we do not prioritize and value campus ministry? What could happen in Every Nation (and in every nation) in the next one hundred years if all our churches continue to equip, empower, mobilize, and fund campus missionaries and campus ministries? What could happen if thousands of Every Nation students earn PhDs and become university professors? What could happen if every church associated with Every Nation makes reaching high school and college campuses their top priority?

NINE

THE BIBLE
AND THE PASSPORT

God had an only Son and He made Him a missionary.
— David Livingstone

Go into all the world and preach the gospel to all creation.

— Jesus (Mark 16:15)

EVERY NATION EXISTS *to honor God by establishing Christ-centered, Spirit-empowered, socially responsible churches and campus ministries in every nation.* We're not in every nation yet, but eventually we will get there, one missionary and one nation at a time.

In the spring of 1980, I was a twenty-year-old business management student at Mississippi State University, and my career path was about to take a dramatic turn toward Asia. Along with some friends, I registered to attend a weekend student mission conference in Atlanta. I don't remember who preached, but I'll never forget his text: Psalm 2:8, "Ask of me, and I will make the nations your inheritance."

As soon as he finished preaching, he told all the students in the room to hit the floor and ask God for a nation. As we put our knees and faces on the floor in prayer, the preacher continued, "Ask God for your inheritance right now. Ask God for a nation."

I don't know what everyone else did, but I did as I was told. I asked God for a nation. And in the holy silence of that moment, I think I heard God speak.

Burma.

With the backdrop of soft music, scattered sobbing, and muted prayers, the preacher continued. "Some of you will become missionaries to the nation God puts in your heart. You will live and die there. Others will become prayer missionaries to a nation. Still others will finance missionaries to a nation."

I had never heard of a prayer missionary or a financial missionary; all I knew was that God seemed to put Burma on my heart. *Was I supposed to quit school and move to Burma? Dang, how do I tell my parents?*

At some point, the preacher clarified that we were not to quit school and buy a plane ticket, but he wanted us to commit to pray for the nation God put on our hearts for the rest of the semester, about eight weeks. I did. And after eight weeks, I still could not get Burma off my heart. I had never met a Burmese person, but after praying for them for a couple of months, I loved them. Prayer will do that to you.

Twenty years later in 1999, I was on a plane with my twelve-year-old son, flying from Manila to Myanmar (the nation formerly known as Burma) to visit our new Every Nation church in Yangoon. It was amazing to finally visit the nation and meet the people for whom I had prayed for so many years. Our Filipino missionaries did a great job, and in a few years passed the leadership baton to capable young Burmese leaders who have taken the church to a new level and helped establish an Every Nation church in neighboring Laos.

A Bible and a Passport

I don't know how Deborah and I knew it, but from the moment we landed in Manila as "accidental missionaries," we knew the church we were planting was called to be a missionary-sending church.

At first glance, our little group of Filipino students seemed to be the least likely bunch of people to go to the nations. Most had never been on an airplane. Only a few had ventured off Manila's home island of Luzon. None of them had passports, much less visas. But God loves to take the "foolish things of the world to shame the wise, and the weak things of the world to shame the strong" (1 Corinthians 1:27). Foolish and weak was a close-to-perfect description of us in those days.

To help these students catch a world vision, we pinned a tattered *National Geographic* world map on the wall of our dark, dingy basement sanctuary. Having been raised Roman Catholic, most of the students were used to dipping their hands in holy water as they entered a church. Rather than holy water, we created a church tradition of putting those same hands on the world map and praying for the world according to Psalm 2:8, "Ask of me, and I will make the nations your inheritance, the ends of the earth your possession."

As these students descended the stairs to worship in the basement (it often reminded me of the early Christians worshiping in the catacombs), they would pray for China, Russia, India, Iran, Israel, and the USA — especially California and Florida, the home of Disneyland and Walt Disney World.

We instinctively knew it was important to instill vision for the world in a new church and in new believers right from the start, so we made world missions the central part of our new believer's foundations class. As soon as a Filipino student surrendered to Christ, we would take them to the last chapter of Matthew's Gospel and explain the Great Commission.

- **All authority in heaven and on earth has been given to me.** First, we would clarify the authority issue. "From now on, Jesus is the final authority in your life. He has *all authority*. You have none. What He says, you do. No complaints. No negotiations. *All authority* means He is Lord. You understand that?" Once we had the authority issue settled, we moved on to the next point.

- **Therefore go and make disciples of all nations.** Our new believer's orientation continued, "In order to be a good Christian, you'll need two things: a Bible and a passport. You'll need a Bible so you can know God. Read it first thing every day. You'll need a passport so you can obey God. You're supposed to *make disciples of all nations*, and you cannot go to the nations without a passport. So if you're serious about being a disciple of Jesus, you will buy a Bible today, and you will fill out a passport application as soon as possible."

That's exactly what we told new believers. And guess what? These poor Filipino students got passports. And they started getting stamps in those passports. First, we sent a short-term mission team to Indonesia, then another to Japan, then another to China. Those teams returned after a couple of weeks. Eventually, we sent teams that didn't return for many years, first to Bangladesh, then to Russia, Latvia, Thailand, Vietnam, Myanmar, Afghanistan, the United Arab Emirates, Spain, and many other nations.

We felt compelled to go to the nations because Jesus died on the cross and with His blood "purchased men for God from every tribe and language and people and nation" (Revelation 5:9). Toward the end of his life, when the apostle John saw a vision of heaven, he saw "a great multitude that no one could count, from every nation, tribe, people and language, standing before the throne and in front of the Lamb" (Revelation 7:9). If heaven is to be populated by people from every tribe, language, and nation, then someone must go to every tribe, language, and nation to preach the Gospel, make disciples, and plant churches.

What Does Every Nation Look Like Today?

When those eleven remaining disciples heard the original Great Commission to "go and make disciples of *all nations*," they took the Gospel to the far corners of the known world. Church tradition tells us that Peter went to Rome, Matthew to Ethiopia, Bartholomew to Turkey and Armenia, Andrew to Greece, Thomas to India, and Jude to Iran. To get to these remote places, they went by foot, by boat, and by camel. That's what "all nations" meant to them, but what does it mean to us today?

Currently, the world holds over seven billion people. Unless you're a math major, seven billion is a difficult number to comprehend. For the math-challenged among us, it might help to imagine the world as a village of only ten people. That village of ten would include one African, one European, one Latino, one North American, and six Asians. Those six Asians would consist of two Chinese, two Indians, one Middle Easterner, and one other Asian (Filipino, Laotian, Thai, and so on).

Four of the ten in our village would own a radio. Two would have cars. Our village would have one phone and one computer. Two villagers would have adequate housing, and only four would have safe drinking water. One would be obese (probably the North American), five would be hungry, and half of our village would live on less than two US dollars per day. And, at the end of the year, one of the ten would have died and two more would be born, increasing our total population to eleven.

Now let's go back to the real world of seven billion people. Here's the current religious breakdown. Thirty-two percent, or two billion people, would tick "Christian" on a survey. That includes Roman Catholics, Orthodox Christians, all variations of Protestants, and even members of semi-Christian fringe groups. Some of these would be whole-hearted followers of Christ; others would be nominal. Twenty-two percent, 1.3 billion people, are Muslims. Like the Christians, some of them are dedicated Muslims, and others not so much. Fifteen percent, or 900 million, are non-religious atheists, agnostics, and skeptics. Fourteen percent, or 800 million, are Hindus. Ten percent practice smaller religions like Judaism, Sikhism, or tribal religions. And seven percent, about 400 million, are Buddhists. That's what our world looks like today.

Somebody Has to Go

Today, the twelve least discipled nations on the planet are Afghanistan, Algeria, Bangladesh, Bhutan, Cambodia, Iran, Nepal, Somalia, Thailand, Turkey, Tunisia, and Yemen. Less than one percent of the people in these nations are Christian. As I write this chapter, we have Every Nation church-planting teams working in seven of these twelve. That's great, but who will go to the other five? Who will pick up a cross and follow Jesus to Algeria, Bhutan, Somalia, Tunisia, and Yemen?

Philanthropist and missionary William Borden (more on William Borden in Chapter 16), who knew a thing or two about mission mobilization, often asked a rhetorical question to drive his point home, "If ten men are carrying a log — nine of them on the little end and one at the heavy end — and you want to help, which end will you lift on?"

The unreached Muslim, Hindu, and Buddhist nations of the world certainly represent the "heavy end" of world missions that very few are trying to carry.

Every Nation churches are currently established in sixty-five nations, but who will go to the remaining 131? Who will help lift the heavy end? Who will go to Morocco, Libya, and Mali in North Africa? Who will go to Chile, Paraguay, and Uruguay in South America? Who will go to Kenya, Rwanda, and Ethiopia in East Africa? Who will go to Norway, Romania, and Italy in Europe? And who will go to Kazakhstan, Tajikistan, and Uzbekistan in Central Asia? Maybe we all need to drop to the floor and ask God for a nation. But before we do, we should adopt the attitude of Nicolaus von Zinzendorf (1700–1760), the founder of the Moravians, who said:

> I have but one passion: It is He, it is He alone. The world is the field and the field is the world; and henceforth that country shall be my home where I can be most used in winning souls for Christ.

But if thousands of people start going to every nation, that's a lot of money for plane tickets.

Somebody Has to Pay

"Dad, we have a great idea," my three young sons beamed with joy.

"What's the great idea, guys?"

"We should all go to America for Christmas this year. Then, we could play in the snow."

Growing up in the tropics, my sons always dreamed of a white Christmas. That would be the American version with white snow, not white sand. They had experienced plenty of white Christmases on beautiful Philippine beaches. But now they wanted the cold stuff.

"That's an interesting idea," I responded, searching for a creative way to tell them it was out of the question. "But, there's one problem."

"What's the one problem, Dad?" they asked in unison, leaning forward, with snowflakes dancing in their eyes.

"It doesn't snow in Mississippi or Georgia where our relatives live."

"That's okay. We can go to Canada too."

"Well, actually, there's another small problem. Somebody has to pay for it!" At some point, as in that moment with my sons, we all learn that dreams are often crushed by financial realities.

It sure sounded like a good idea to them. Hop on a jet. Fly to the States for a few days. Get piles of Christmas gifts from adoring grandparents, uncles, aunts, and cousins. Go to Canada. Throw a few snowballs. Be back at home in Manila in a week. No problem.

But there was a problem, the age-old problem called money. Coming up with a good Christmas vacation idea is the easy part. Paying for it is the hard part. Someone has to count the cost, take responsibility, and pay the bill. The more nations we want to reach, and the more missionaries we want to send, the more it will cost.

While I don't want anyone to ever go as unprepared and underfunded as we did in 1984, I'm also not suggesting that we sit around and do nothing until we have all the money we need. At some point, we have to take a bold, sacrificial leap of faith if we want to go to every nation. In his excellent book, *Movements that Change the World*, Steve Addison addresses the role of faith:

> Church history is not made by well-financed, well-resourced individuals and institutions. History is made by men and women of faith who have met with the living God. Without faith it is impossible to please God.

The Spirit Is Willing, but the Wallet Is Weak
During a recent conversation with a well-known mission leader, we discussed our common passion for establishing missionary-sending churches. We rejoiced that so many believers are willing to go. We lamented that so few churches seem willing to send.

The lack of mission funding is a global problem and not one unique to a particular region of the world. Countless believers in many countries have caught the Great Commission vision. They're ready to go to every nation with the Gospel. But as I told my son about his Christmas vacation plans, there's only one problem: Somebody has to pay for it! World mission is expensive.

Two thousand years ago, the apostle Paul asked,

How, then, can they call on the one they have not believed in? And how can they believe in the one of whom they have not heard? And how can they hear without someone preaching to them. And how can they preach unless they are sent? (Romans 10:14–15)

I'll add a few more questions to Paul's list: And how can they be sent unless someone gives? And how can they buy plane tickets unless churches take up mission offerings? And how can they be supported unless pastors make world missions a priority in their local church budgets?

As important as money is to the fulfillment of the Great Commission, something is even more important.

Somebody Has to Pray

All religious people know that prayer is important. But what should we pray for? Jesus was crystal clear about what He wants on our prayer list: "My house will be called a house of prayer for all nations" (Mark 11:17). Don't miss those last three words, "for all nations." I know we pray for friends and family, but do we pray for our missionaries in all nations?

On January 19, 1888, in Toronto, historic Knox Church was filled to capacity. Excitement was in the air. A young man and his new bride were addressing their home church for the last time before being sent to an African mission field known then as "The White Man's Grave."

"My wife and I have a strange dread in going," the young man spoke soberly, citing the classic William Carey rope illustration. "We feel much as if we were going down into a pit. We are willing to take the risk and go if you, our home circle, will promise to hold the ropes."

This brave young couple knew that they were engaging in dangerous business. They knew the stakes were high, and they couldn't do it alone. They were asking for help. In the inspiration and anointing of the moment, the people responded heroically. Everyone present promised to pray for their missionaries. I'm sure they were sincere.

Unfortunately, sincerity just doesn't cut it on the front line.

Within two years, his wife and new baby were buried in "The White Man's Grave" in Africa. When this brave young missionary contracted the same fatal fever and realized he was dying, he decided to return to Canada. As soon as he arrived, he attended the Wednesday night Knox Church prayer meeting. No one noticed as he slipped in and sat on the back pew. As the prayer meeting dutifully crawled to its close, he went forward. The people were in complete shock as this emaciated, broken shell of a man began to speak.

> I am your missionary. My wife and child are buried in Africa, and I have come home to die. This evening I listened anxiously as you prayed, for some mention of your missionary to see if you were keeping your promise, but in vain! You prayed for everything connected with yourselves and your home church, but you forgot your missionary. I see now why I am a failure as a missionary. It is because you have failed to hold the ropes!

Could the prayerlessness of his home church really be the reason he lost his wife and child? "Holding the ropes" is serious business, especially when the Gospel is being taken into hostile territory.

All of us, I'm sure, have promised to hold some ropes for missionaries who have responded to the command to forsake all and follow Christ. Their obedience has landed them in distant and sometimes dangerous lands. They're doing their part. How about us? Are we faithfully holding the ropes?

The Best Way to Experience the Presence of God

Two years ago, I was enjoying a peacefully silent Christmas morning, a far cry from the frenzied, raucous, joyful mornings when the boys were much younger. As it softly snowed outside, I was reading the book of Acts and thinking about "Immanuel, God with us" (Matthew 1:23).

Do you ever feel far from God, like Immanuel is not particularly close? We all do at times. Acts 23:11 says, "The following night *the Lord stood near* Paul." Why did He *stand near* Paul but often seems to stand so far from us?

Maybe because we live such safe and comfortable lives, we don't think we need Him close all the time. Paul's life was so unsafe and uncomfortable that he needed God close in order to survive each day. Here's what prompted the Lord to stand near Paul: "The dispute [between the Pharisees and Sadducees] became *so violent that the commander was afraid Paul would be torn to pieces* by them. He ordered the troops to go down and take him away from them by force and bring him into the barracks" (Acts 23:10).

Do you want to experience God's nearness? Simple. Get out of your comfort zone, get on mission, take a leap of faith, and watch what happens — religious people will try to kill you, and the Lord will stand near.

The Hundred-Year Question

The Great Commission starts by clarifying the authority issue; then Jesus calls us to disciple all nations. Finally, He promises His presence: "Surely I am with you always to the very end of the age" (Matthew 28:20). So, the best way to experience the fullness of His presence is to *go and make disciples of all nations.*

What will Every Nation look like in one hundred years if we continue to *go and make disciples of all nations*? What will happen to us in one hundred years if we do fail to pray, give, and go to all nations?

VALUES

- *Lordship*
- *Evangelism*
- *Discipleship*
- *Leadership*
- *Family*

TEN

THEOLOGICAL MALPRACTICE

There is not one square inch of the entire creation about which Jesus Christ does not cry out, 'This is mine! This belongs to me!'
— Abraham Kuyper, Dutch Prime Minister

Why do you call me, "Lord, Lord," and do not do what I say?
— Jesus (Luke 6:46)

YOU CANNOT WALK INTO A BANK anywhere in Southeast Asia without being greeted by armed security guards. These guards have jobs for two reasons: (1) the money in the bank and (2) the thieves who want to steal the money in the bank. Every time I walk past an armed security guard, I think about Paul's word to Timothy to "guard the good deposit . . . with the help of the Holy Spirit" (2 Timothy 1:13–14).

Like Timothy, every ministry has a good deposit that must be guarded. I look at our core values as the good deposit we must guard together. The five Every Nation core values define who we are as a movement of churches. They must be guarded with the help of the Holy Spirit or they will be lost. Whether we're planting a new church, building a campus ministry, or developing a music team, these five core values describe how we build.

1. **Lordship.** Because Jesus is King of kings and Lord of lords, we believe that wholehearted submission to God's will and His Word is the starting point and the foundation of spiritual growth.

2. **Evangelism.** Because "God so loved the world that He gave His one and only Son, that whoever believes in Him shall not perish but have eternal life" (John 3:6), we are passionate about preaching the Gospel and doing ministry in a way that engages people outside of the Christian faith.

3. **Discipleship.** Because we are called to make disciples, our primary focus is establishing biblical foundations, equipping believers to minister, and empowering disciples to make disciples.

4. **Leadership.** Because we are called to establish churches in every nation, we are committed to leadership development. We are intentionally multi-generational and we deliberately create opportunities and platforms for next-generation leaders.

5. **Family.** Because family is the foundation and validation of ministry, we refuse to sacrifice our marriages and our children on the altars of temporal ministry success. And because God has called us to be a church family, we embrace community and reject the concept of disposable relationships.

The rest of this chapter will examine our first and foundational core value: the Lordship of Christ. Subsequent chapters will deal with the four other core values that logically spring from Lordship.

Jesus Is Lord!

If I heard it once, I heard it a million times. "If Christ is not Lord *of* all, He is not Lord *at* all." That's how Ron Musselman, the Presbyterian youth pastor who led me to Christ, started and ended every Bible study, every discipleship group, and every prayer meeting. At least it seems like he did. Whether Ron actually repeated that phrase every day or not, he definitely drove home the fact that Jesus is Lord, not just Savior. I'm thankful that the Lordship of Christ was the starting point of my Christian journey. From day one, Ron taught me that Jesus gave His all on the cross and that He demands and deserves my all. He taught me that the only reasonable response to what Christ did for me was to fully surrender my life to Him, every day, all the time. Ron taught me that Jesus is Lord. It is who He is. And if I want a relationship with Him, I have to relate to Him as Lord. I cannot change who He is. He is Lord. My only option is to submit to or reject His Lordship.

John MacArthur, in *The Gospel According to Jesus,* explained Lordship much the same way Ron explained it to me.

> We do not "make" Christ Lord; He is Lord! Those who will not receive Him as Lord are guilty of rejecting Him. "Faith" that rejects His sovereign authority is really unbelief. Conversely, acknowledging His Lordship is no more a human work than repentance or faith itself. In fact, it is an important element of divinely produced saving faith, not something added to faith.

James addressed this same Lordship issue with these words:

> But someone will say, 'You have faith; I have deeds.' Show me your faith without deeds, and I will show you my faith by what I do. You believe that there is one God. Good! Even the demons believe that — and shudder." (James 2:18–19)

He was certainly not arguing against salvation by grace through faith. What he was contesting was the idea that one can have genuine faith, but no corresponding good deeds.

When we reject the Lordship of Christ, we make up a Jesus who is less than the Jesus of Scripture. Liberalism makes Jesus a great moral teacher, minus the miracles. Liberation Theology makes Jesus a revolutionary hero, rather than a crucified and resurrected Christ. Legalism makes Jesus seem like a self-righteous Pharisee, rather than a gracious Savior.

In the first century, many people had incomplete and inaccurate ideas as to who Jesus was. To clarify the real identity of Jesus, Peter ended his Pentecost sermon with these words, "Therefore, let all Israel be assured of this: God made this Jesus, whom you crucified, both Lord and Christ" (Acts 2:36). So if we want to receive Him, we must receive Him as Lord and Christ, because that's who He is.

But receiving Him as Lord is only the start; we must also continue to walk in His Lordship throughout our spiritual journey. Paul told the Colossians, "Just as you received Christ Jesus as Lord, *continue* to live in him" (Colossians 2:6).

The Honest Toddler

Here's a funny story that captures the heart of Lordship. About twenty years ago, my wife and I were attempting to teach our three sons some basic table manners. At the time, they were seven, five, and three. We had one simple rule: no one leaves the table until they finish all their food and have parental permission to leave. This new policy worked great — for two days.

"Jonathan, sit down," I told my three-year-old as he tiptoed away from the table, trying to look invisible.

"But I want some more milk," Jonathan replied as he inched his way toward the refrigerator door.

"Jonathan, you know you're not supposed to get up from the table until you finish eating."

"But I need more milk, see?" As he said, "see," he turned his semi-empty cup upside-down, pouring milk down his leg.

"Jonathan, sit down. Now. Okay?"

"But I'm thirsty."

I sensed this might go on forever, so I changed my approach, and foolishly attempted to reason with a three-year-old: "Jonathan, who's the boss here?"

Now, my honest toddler stopped, looked me square in the face, and said, "Me and you, Dad."

As soon as these words escaped his mouth, we had our own private laughing revival. Deborah and Jonathan's brothers thought it was the funniest thing they had ever heard.

I suppose it is funny when a three-year-old, with milk dripping down his leg, claims to have equal authority with his dad. However, it's not so funny when people who are two years old in the Lord claim to have equal authority with God. Nor is it funny when God says not to get up from the table and we get up anyway — without His permission. And it's not funny when God asks, "Who's the boss?" and we answer, "Me and you, God."

Christians need to get one thing straight: Lordship means there is a boss, and it's not you. God is the boss. He makes the rules. He calls the shots. Our job is simply to listen and obey.

Avoiding Theological Malpractice

A long time ago, Jesus asked a bunch of spiritual three-year-olds a piercing question: "Why do you call me Lord, Lord, and do not do what I say?" (Luke 6:46). Good question.

I should have asked Jonathan, "Why do you call me Dad, Dad, and do not do what I say?"

In the book, *Almost Christian*, Princeton University theology professor Kenda Creasy Dean uses the phrase "theological malpractice" to describe the absence of Lordship in homes and churches.

> What if the blasé religiosity of most American teenagers is not the result of poor communication, but the result of excellent communication of a watered-down Gospel so devoid of God's self-giving love in Jesus Christ, so immune to the sending love of the Holy Spirit that it might not be Christianity at all? What if the church models a way of life that asks not for passionate surrender, but for ho-hum assent? What if we are preaching moral affirmation, a feel-better faith, and a hands-off God instead of the decisively involved, impossibly loving, radically sending God of Abraham and Mary, who desired us enough to enter creation in Jesus Christ and whose Spirit is active in the church and in the world today? If this is the case — if *theological malpractice* explains teenagers' half-hearted religious identities — then perhaps most young people practice Moralistic Therapeutic Deism not because they reject Christianity, but because this is the only "Christianity" they know.

Because of rampant "theological malpractice" in the church today, many say, "Jesus is Lord" but ignore what He says. Hopefully, we can avoid this with a better understanding of what "Jesus is Lord" actually means.

- **"Jesus is Lord" is a theological statement.** Jesus spoke of the eternal ramifications of His Lordship when He said, "Not everyone who says to me, 'Lord, Lord' will enter the kingdom of heaven" (Matthew 7:21). You do the math. If they don't enter the kingdom of heaven, where do they go? Paul connects salvation with the Lordship of Christ when he writes, "If you confess with your mouth, 'Jesus is Lord' and believe in your heart that God raised him from the dead, you will be saved" (Romans 10:9). The Greek word translated "Lord" is used over six thousand times in the Septuagint (the Greek Old Testament) for the name of God or Yahweh. This means that the "Lord God" who spoke to Abraham, Moses, Elijah, and Elijah in the Old Testament is the same "Lord" that Paul says we must confess for salvation. In other words, saying Jesus is Lord is saying that Jesus is the Old Testament God who came in human flesh in Bethlehem. In his book, *I Call It Heresy*, A.W. Tozer sees the clear connection between Lordship and salvation: "The Lord will not save those whom He cannot command. He will not divide his offices. You cannot believe on a half-Christ. We take Him for what He is — the anointed Saviour and Lord."

- **"Jesus is Lord" is a political statement.** In England, they might greet one another with a hearty, "God save the Queen." During Nazi Germany, it was, *"Heil, Hitler!"* In ancient Rome, the greeting was, "Caesar is Lord," meaning Caesar is divine. That last statement was more political than theological for the ancient Romans. Of course, the early Christians refused to call Caesar lord, so they greeted one another, "Jesus is Lord." They were not persecuted primarily because of the theological implications of that statement. They were burned alive because "Jesus is Lord" was seen as an anti-Caesar political statement. The chief priests understood the danger of being politically disloyal to Caesar. When Pilot presented Jesus to the crowd saying, "Here is your king," the chief priests immediately shouted the politically correct response, "Crucify him!" and "We have no king but Caesar" (John 19:14–15).

- **"Jesus is Lord" is a personal statement.** It is not enough to be theologically or politically correct. Until Jesus becomes my personal Lord, I have missed the point. Nothing is more personal than the heart. The apostle Peter wrote, "But *in your hearts* set apart Christ as Lord" (1 Peter 3:15). Lordship starts in the heart, and then invades every area of life.

Lord, Lord, Nevermind

It's a sad fact that countless people claim to follow Jesus, but don't do what He says. Why is this? I can think of four reasons.

1. **Some are sincere, but ignorant.** I was like this for the first three years of my Christian life concerning water baptism. I sincerely desired to fully follow God's Word, but I was ignorant about believer's baptism. As soon I understood what the Bible taught, I obeyed and was baptized.

2. **Some are sincere, but independent.** People like this seem to have a sincere desire to follow Jesus, but are not part of a discipleship group and are not connected to a church community. Christianity is not a solo sport. We need one another. I thank God that the Presbyterian youth pastor who led me to Christ also included me in his small discipleship group. If I had failed to get connected to a church community that was committed to my spiritual growth, I'm sure I would have called Him Lord while disobeying everything He said.

3. **Some are sincere, but in bondage.** Some really want to serve God but are bound by cords of past or present sin. They say, "Lord, Lord" but continue to fall into the same pattern of destructive habits. They are in bondage. The good news is that the truth sets us free. Sometimes freedom comes in an instant; other times it requires the long, tedious process of discipleship and renewing the mind. No matter if it's a short or long process, whomever the Son sets free, is "free indeed" (John 8:36).

4. **Some are not sincere at all.** Finally, some people have no intention of obeying God. They are counterfeit converts, spiritual knock-offs ("copy watches" for my readers in Asia). I don't know why they even bother to say, "Lord, Lord." These are the religious phonies that Don Carson referred to in his commentary, *Basics for Believers: An Exposition of Philippians*:

   I would like to buy about three dollars worth of Gospel, please. Not too much — just enough to make me happy, but not so much that I get addicted. I don't want so much Gospel that I learn to really hate covetousness and lust. I certainly don't want so much that I start to love my enemies, cherish self-denial, and contemplate missionary service in some alien culture. I want ecstasy, not repentance; I want transcendence, not transformation. I would like to be cherished by some nice, forgiving, broad-minded people, but I myself don't want to love those from different races — especially if they smell. I would like enough Gospel to make my family secure and my children well behaved, but not so much that I find my ambitions redirected or my giving too greatly enlarged. I would like about three dollars worth of Gospel, please.

I used to think that anyone who said, "Lord, Lord," and didn't consistently obey was a phony. Not anymore. I realize the there are some people who need teaching, some who need discipleship, and some who need deliverance. Some people simply need to repent. But sadly, the message of repentance and surrendering to the Lordship of Christ seems to be missing in many churches around the world.

The Hundred-Year Question

In his classic book, *The Pursuit of God*, A.W. Tozer described the rationale of Lordship:

> God, being who and what He is, and we, being who and what we are, the only thinkable relation between us is one of *full Lordship* on His part and *complete submission* on ours. We owe Him every honor that is in our power to give Him. Our everlasting grief lies in giving Him anything less.

And that brings us back to the story of my three-year-old son, his empty milk cup, and my question to him: "Who's the boss?" If you ever hear a still, small voice asking: "Who's the boss here anyway?" remember, the answer is not: "You and me, Lord."

What will we become in one hundred years if we do not live and preach the Lordship of Christ? What will happen in Every Nation churches and campus ministries if we continue to preach and live the Lordship of Christ?

ELEVEN

DANGEROUS DECISIONS

> *How much do you have to hate somebody to believe that*
> *everlasting life is possible, and not tell them about it?*
> — Atheist Penn Jillette,

> *Pray for me, that whenever I speak, words may be*
> *given me so that I will fearlessly make known the*
> *mystery of the gospel.*
> — Apostle Paul (Ephesians 6:19)

JESUS HAD SOME EXPLAINING TO DO. The religious leaders had accused Him of welcoming tax collectors and sinners, then sitting down to actually *eat* with them. All of it was highly inappropriate behavior — at least, improper *religious* behavior.

"Guilty as charged," He might have said. "But you have a wrong perspective on your religion, which has caused you to miss the point altogether."

Jesus responded to them with three parables. The first one is about a shepherd with one hundred sheep. One sheep is lost, so the shepherd leaves the ninety-nine and goes after the lost one until he finds it. The second story is about a woman who lost a coin. She searches for it until she finds it too. Both the woman and the shepherd are thrilled over finding what was lost. Jesus then said, "I tell you that in the same way, there will be more joy in heaven over one sinner who repents than over ninety-nine righteous persons who need no repentance" (Luke 15:7). And the third story, the most famous of all, is about a lost son who returns to his father. The father then throws a huge welcome-home party for his prodigal son.

Unlike the religious leaders of His day, Jesus was seeking and searching for lost souls and not particularly worried about getting dirty by association. Why do religious people have such a difficult time with this? Why don't we leave the ninety-nine and pursue the one? The reasons for this may be many layers deep, but it seems to me that it's often more about fear than anything else. We're afraid that we won't know what to say or how to relate; afraid that we might be more infected by what the "sinners" have than the other way around. Sometimes we're simply afraid because some very dangerous people are out there.

Boldly Stepping into the Danger Zone

My good friend, Rocky, is our Every Nation leader in Bangladesh. We call him Rocky because he's a former boxing champion, and because most of us can't properly pronounce his Bengali name. His nation is one of the least Christian nations on the planet. It's also on all the top-ten lists of nations that persecute Christians. But Rocky is what I call "crazy bold." Most of my Chinese friends are bold like Rocky. So are my friends who serve in the Middle East. Now that I think about it, most of my friends seem to be crazy bold.

Rocky and his team of Bangladeshi leaders do city-to-city ministry like the early Methodist circuit riders who led congregations in multiple cities. One morning while "circuit riding" in another city, Rocky received a phone call at five o'clock from a friend.

Friend: "Can you meet with a very influential local leader this morning?"

Rocky: "It's five a.m.! Why are you calling me so early?"

Friend: "We have to meet now; before the sun comes up. This guy is known as a very, very dangerous man."

Rocky: "Okay. Who is he, and where do we meet?"

Rocky's friend briefly described the chief *imam* in the district they were visiting. This man had enormous influence over thousands of people who desperately needed to hear the Gospel.

Rocky was scheduled to lead a discipleship meeting with a group of people at 6:30 that morning. After a quick prayer, he headed toward the agreed-upon rendezvous point to meet this influential imam. Rocky didn't tell his wife exactly where he was going or who he was meeting, but he left her a cryptic text message that fully communicated the potential danger he was facing: "I'm going to meet a man at the seaside, please pray for me till I return." Over the years, Rocky's wife has gotten used to cryptic messages, dangerous meetings, and emergency intercession.

Rocky met his friend and the imam near the seaside under the designated pine tree, and they began to talk. At first, the imam was very tense — not smiling, eyes darting around. Rocky honored him for being a renowned religious leader in the community, then listened attentively to his life story. As a child, the imam had studied for many years in a *madrasa* (an Islamic school for boys) and afterwards had joined the mission of Al-Qaeda. He eventually went to a military training camp in Pakistan and then to Afghanistan as an insurgent, a jihadist fighting a religious war for Allah. He went on for half an hour, speaking proudly of how he had killed many foreign infidels in service to Allah. In Pakistan at one point, he served as bodyguard for Osama Bin Laden. Eventually, he was wounded and returned home for medical treatment where he took his current position as an imam at the mosque.

The two teachers, Rocky and the imam, dove deep into a theological discussion about Allah, Islam, good and evil, love and hate. The conversation was passionate and honest. Eventually, the imam admitted that he never thought about Allah in the way Rocky presented God. Rocky asked him if he wanted to follow the God of the Bible who loves sinners but hates sin. Finally, he humbled himself, sat down on the ground, repented, and asked Allah to forgive him. That day, he counted the cost, picked up his cross, and became a follower of Jesus. Rocky heard later that he went straight to the district commissioner and resigned from his job as a district chief imam. Today, he's still carrying his cross, following Jesus, and making disciples.

Good thing Rocky was willing to leave the ninety-nine in order to meet the one who was lost, deceived, and dangerous.

The Ninety-Nine-and-the-One Strategy

Sometimes God does not count like we do. His value system turns ours upside-down. The story of the shepherd and the lost sheep in Luke 15 is one of those strange math stories. Jesus poses a question: "Does he (the shepherd) not leave the ninety-nine to go after the missing one?" In modern-day motivational language, we would phrase the question like this: "Is the glass ninety-nine percent full or one percent empty?" While we immediately assume the right answer to be "ninety-nine percent full," apparently Jesus seemed to focus more on the missing one. Then He adds, "There will be more rejoicing in heaven over one sinner who repents than over ninety-nine righteous persons who do not need to repent" (Luke 15:6).

No matter how many ways we look at this story, it always betrays common sense. The shepherd left all the non-lost sheep "in the open country" (Luke 15:4). Why jeopardize the ninety-nine in an effort to search for that one, even though you might not be able to rescue it? For church leaders, it really doesn't make practical sense in terms of budget, staffing, and focus. It's hard to justify a strategy that seems to value one more than ninety-nine. Like many things that Jesus said, it doesn't make sense because, like the Pharisees, we often have a wrong perspective.

The Ninety-Nine-and-the-One strategy only makes sense if we keep two spiritual concepts in mind:

1. **Grace.** The grace of God is not to be consumed only on ourselves but freely extended to others who are no more deserving than us. Don't forget that God loves Roman tax collectors, Jewish Pharisees, and Islamic imams every bit as much as He loves the mega-church senior pastor and the missional-church lead pastor. Grace is the only reason we're not in that lineup of sinners on the last day.

2. **Maturity.** In the next chapter, we'll look at a concept I call "The Myth of Maturity." For now, it's enough to say that the myth is assuming that people need to be experts in order to begin ministering to others. The truth is, Christian maturity is the *result* of ministering

the Gospel, not a *prerequisite* for it. The faith journey is a learn-by-doing endeavor.

Leaving 2,000 and Searching for 20,000

In 1984, we planted a church in the Philippines, and in six years, we saw it grow to two thousand people in two Manila locations. It looked pretty good on the surface, but we had significant flaws in the foundation—not so much in what we were doing but in the way we were thinking. Those flaws were, nonetheless, things that certainly would have limited our health and growth over time. So in order to more effectively reach the unchurched, we made a monumental strategy shift in the early nineties, one that enabled us to continue growing from two thousand to over seventy-five thousand through the following two decades. We made the decision to organize and lead the church around small, outwardly focused discipleship groups. This decision was based on the conviction that engaging non-believers is the first step in the discipleship process.

With two thousand people already attending, the staff wanted to know, "How do we get everyone in the church involved?"

My immediate and constant answer was, "We won't get everyone involved. Some will buy in. Many will not. This is about the twenty thousand we've not yet reached, not the two thousand we've already reached." For me, the driving passion was the fact that we were in a city surrounded by millions who have never heard the Gospel. We had to figure out how to reach them. So we built a discipleship infrastructure for twenty thousand when our church attendance was only two thousand.

That was our way of "leaving the ninety-nine" and going after the lost one. Biblical disciple-making begins with a search for the lost, not the gathering of the already found.

Leaving ninety-nine to search for one is such an improbable illustration that no one other than Jesus would have ever come up with it. What that idea suggests is an outward rather than inward focus in our congregations, our programming, and our ministry priorities. It presumes that members are mindful of the grace of God and that they don't need years of training before they can minister.

We still have people from that original group of two thousand. Those who remained are still around because they got off the bench and started engaging their communities. More importantly, new generations of disciples simply saw outreach as normal Christianity.

I am the first to say that we cannot simply download and install a strategy from another culture and expect it to work. Each local church has to crack their own missional code. But there are some underlying Kingdom principles that always apply. The Ninety-Nine-and-the-One strategy is based on a universal principle that teaches us to have an outward rather than an inward focus. Engaging your community and culture may not look anything like what we did in Manila. But let me put it as straightforwardly as I can—if a significant percentage of a congregation does not begin to intentionally and strategically engage the culture and community in an ongoing way, then the church will become increasingly inward-focused, consumer-driven, and spectator-oriented. The mission will be all about endlessly feeding or entertaining the ninety-nine while ignoring the one.

What Engaging Culture and Community Does Not Mean

To what extent are the people in our local churches engaging their culture and communities for Christ? Here's what that means and what it does not mean:

- **It does not just mean pastors, evangelists, and staff engaging culture and community.** Full-time ministers certainly must engage the culture and community, but their biblical job description is "to equip God's people for works of service" (Ephesians 4:11–12). They set the examples, and they lead the way, but the critical question relates to what degree our non-paid church members engage their culture and community for Christ.

- **It does not mean that members of Every Nation churches become "community-minded do-gooders."** Our members could and do wind up serving people at the point of their most basic human needs and do so without respect to their response, religious background, or ability to give back. But they must always do it in the name of Christ and as a witness to the Gospel. The goal in engaging culture and community is to preach the Gospel.

- **It does not mean ushering, serving in kids' ministry, or other church departments.** Serving in the local church is important, but it's not the same as engaging the culture and community. Serving the local church is actually serving ourselves, not our communities.

What engaging culture and community does mean is sharing the Gospel with the lost. While it has become popular to do good deeds "with no strings attached," Paul intentionally attached the Gospel to everything he did as he engaged his culture. Notice his stated motive:

Though I am free and belong to no one, I have made myself a slave to everyone, to win as many as possible. To the Jews I became like a Jew, to win the Jews. To those under the law I became like one under the law (though I myself am not under the law), so as to win those under the law. To those not having the law I became like one not having the law (though I am not free from God's law but am under Christ's law), so as to win those not having the law. To the weak I became weak, to win the weak. I have become all things to all people so that by all possible means I might save some. I do all this for the sake of the gospel, that I may share in its blessings. (1 Corinthians 9:19–23)

What Is the Gospel?

Several years ago, I had a strange conversation with a campus missionary. I mentioned something about the need to equip church members to share the Gospel. He responded, "But what is the Gospel?"

As I began to answer his question, I quickly realized it was not a question at all. He was not looking for clarification. He was challenging the traditional understanding of the Gospel. Through blogs and podcasts, he now had a new understanding of the Gospel, an understanding that apparently few in the history of the church had ever grasped. I tried my best to get him back on track, but he "knew too much" and would not listen. I'm not sure what he's doing today.

With that conversation in mind, I think it might be necessary in this chapter on evangelism to clearly explain what I mean by preaching the Gospel.

The apostle Paul wrote, "Jews demand signs and Greeks look for wisdom, but we preach Christ crucified: a stumbling block to Jews and foolishness to Gentiles" (1 Corinthians 1:22–23). That's another way of saying that the Gospel doesn't make sense to sinners trying to work their way to heaven (Jews) any more than it does to those who don't see themselves as sinners at all (Greeks).

Consider those two opposite objections — some reject the Gospel because it demands that they acknowledge that they are, in fact, sinners in need of a Savior. Others reject the Gospel because it requires them to acknowledge that no amount of good works can atone for any past sin. The truth is so contrary to our sin and self-sufficiency that it's no wonder every generation has to reaffirm the Gospel. The difficulty we have with the Gospel is not because it's complicated, but because it offends our pride.

In his little book, *A Primer on Justification*, Professor John Gerstner provides a simple way of understanding the biblical Gospel formula — justification by grace through faith alone. Gerstner describes several historic "departures" from the Gospel. Here's my summary of Gerstner's concept:

FIRST DEPARTURE: LIBERALISM
Works = Justification – Faith
Liberalism in this context has nothing to do with politics. Theologically, it usually refers to a retreat from faith in the incarnation, resurrection, virgin birth, and particularly the atonement (blood sacrifice to take away our sin). This particular departure from the Gospel results in people believing they are justified by good behavior, without a need to receive Christ's blood atonement by faith. In other words, good works equal justification before God without the need of (minus) faith.

SECOND DEPARTURE: ANTINOMIANISM
Faith = Justification – Works

Antinomianism literally means "without law." Theologically, it refers to the belief that individuals are justified before God by faith alone without any corresponding change in moral or ethical restriction or in behavior. Antinomians depart from the Gospel by omitting repentance, Lordship, and sanctification from the formula. Gerstner says that for antinomians, justification by faith becomes "just a vacation by faith." Thus, in the antinomian Gospel, faith equals justification without the need of (minus) works.

THIRD DEPARTURE: LEGALISM
Faith + Works = Justification

Gerstner actually called this the Roman Catholic departure, but legalism is certainly not exclusive to Catholicism. I've known plenty of legalistic Presbyterians, Pentecostals, Baptists, and incarnational/missional/organic churches that add their own version of good works to faith. And yes, I've encountered and confronted legalism in our own churches, and in my own life. According to Gerstner, traditional Roman Catholicism is a partial departure, because Catholics have been faithful to preserve key elements of truth about the Person of Christ — the incarnation, divinity, resurrection, second coming, etc.

The legalism departure, whether Catholic or Charismatic, happens when traditions and additional requirements are added to the Gospel. For a Catholic, that might include prayer to the saints, the deification of Mary, and numerous other non-biblical beliefs and traditions that have been added to the simple Gospel. It's easy for Pentecostals and Presbyterians to point fingers at the Catholic add-ons, while adding their own traditions. Rather than praying the rosary, Charismatics pray in tongues and confess the Word, thinking that adding those works to their faith might get God to like them more. Some Pentecostals think that their dress codes make them God's favorites, and some of my Baptist friends assume that if they avoid bad movies and protest moral decay in the culture, then God will certainly bless them.

In all these departures, the true Gospel is diluted by the additives, leading people to wrongly believe that justification is at least partially dependent on their good works. Consequently, their formula for justification becomes: Faith plus works equals justification.

THE GOSPEL
Faith = Justification + Works
The apostle Paul wrote to the Ephesians,

> For it is by grace you have been saved, through faith — and this is not from yourselves, it is the gift of God — not by works, so that no one can boast. For we are God's handiwork, created in Christ Jesus to do good works, which God prepared in advance for us to do. (Ephesians 2:8–10)

When we put faith in Christ as the whole and sole means of our salvation, God reckons us righteous. That's another way of saying that He *imputes* His righteousness to our account and our sins are forgiven. But that's not all. Christ also *imparts* His righteousness by the Presence and Person of the Holy Spirit. In other words, we're transformed from within, and as a result, we live outwardly transformed lives. We are saved *for* good works, not *by* them. Or to put it in the words of F.F. Bruce, "Justification is by faith alone, but the faith that justifies is not alone."

I love the way Charles Spurgeon explained the role of good works in his 1858 sermon, "A Free Salvation."

> Do you find fault with good works? Not at all! Suppose I see a man building a house and he were fool enough to lay the foundation with roofing tiles. If I should say, "My dear Man, I do not like these roofing tiles to be put into the foundation," you would not say I found fault with the roofing tiles, but that I found fault with the man for putting them in the wrong place! Let him put good solid masonry at the bottom — and then when the house is built he may put on as many roofing tiles as he likes! So with good works and ceremonies — they will not do for a foundation. The foundation must be built of more solid stuff. Our hope

must be built on nothing less than Jesus' blood and righteousness — and when we have built a foundation with that, we may have as many good works as we like — the more the better! But for a foundation, good works are fickle and feeble things — and he that uses them will see his house totter to the ground.

The Hundred-Year Question

I've watched dozens of evangelism fads come and go in my years in ministry. Some have been effective, others not so much. I first heard the Gospel through *Evangelism Explosion* (EE). We planted the church in Manila using an EE spinoff called *The Two Question Test*. I have also received *Four Spiritual Laws* training and *Contagious Christian* training. A new tool that is being used on campuses and cities all over the world is *The God Test*. I'm sure many more tools will be created in the coming years. In addition to good tools and training, I think we should all take to heart what Bill Hybels says about evangelism in his book, *Just Walk Across the Room.*

> I'm more convinced than ever that the absolute *highest* value in personal evangelism is staying attuned to and cooperative with the Holy Spirit. You read it right. The only thing you need in order to sustain an effective approach to evangelism year after year is an ear fine-tuned to the prompting of the Holy Spirit.

What will happen in the next one hundred years if we do not follow the prompting of the Holy Spirit and intentionally engage our communities? What will happen if we do not believe and preach the true Gospel? On the other hand, what will happen in and through Every Nation in the next one hundred years if we respond to the promptings of the Holy Spirit and share the Gospel with our neighbors? What will happen if we embrace the Ninety-Nine-and-the-One strategy in our communities?

TWELVE

DOMINO DISCIPLESHIP

> *Discipleship is relationship.*
> — Joey Bonifacio, *The Lego Principle*

> *And the things you have heard me say in the presence*
> *of many witnesses entrust to reliable people who will*
> *also be qualified to teach others.*
> — Apostle Paul (2 Timothy 2:2)

WHEN I MET GREG WARK over twenty years ago, he was a pastor in San Diego. Today, he serves as a missionary to the United States military, police, and other first-responders who stand in harm's way. As the founder and director of Force Ministries, Greg has made disciples among groups of elite military personnel, including Green Berets, Navy SEALS, midshipmen at the U.S. Naval Academy, and others.

On one occasion, Greg let me come with him to the United States Naval Academy in Annapolis where I met Lieutenant Commander Kurt Parsons, a highly decorated Naval officer and combat pilot with several tours of duty in Iraq, Afghanistan, and other undisclosed locations. When I met Kurt, he taught ethics and leadership at the Academy and was a company officer responsible for over 150 midshipmen. Most importantly, at the time, Kurt was also the leader of Force Ministries' discipleship training for midshipmen at the Academy.

Impromptu Discipleship Moments
Walking through that historic campus with Greg and Kurt was an unforgettable experience. I wondered if we would ever make it to Kurt's

office because about a dozen impromptu discipleship moments happened as we strolled around. By "discipleship moment," I mean encouragement, instruction, and accountability regarding spiritual disciplines and personal life.

"Good afternoon, Andrew." Kurt seemed to know every student we passed.

"Good afternoon, sir."

"How did you do on that chemistry exam?"

"Killed it, sir."

"Good. You been reading your Bible?"

"Yes, sir."

We continued our slow walk to Kurt's office, until we met another student ten steps later.

"Carlos, how's your grandmother doing?"

"Better, sir. Thanks for asking, sir."

"I've been praying for her, and for you."

"Thank you, sir. I need prayer, sir."

"I hope to see you at the Bible study later."

"I'll be there, sir."

Other officers passed the same students, with little connection. But Kurt seemed to know something about every young man and woman on that campus.

Beyond the required military formality, I could tell those young men and women deeply loved Kurt and had enormous respect for him. Every one of them would have followed him into combat without hesitation. The eagerness to learn, willingness to sacrifice, and dedication to serve among these future Naval and Marine Corps officers was not just impressive, it was humbling and inspiring. These Force Ministries men and women at the United States Naval Academy take very seriously the call to discipleship and the heavy responsibility of the Great Commission.

In that place, meeting those Force Ministries disciples and watching them interact with Kurt, I couldn't help but think about how Jesus chose the Twelve. What kind of selection process would you conduct for such an elite squad of disciples, commissioned with the sole responsibility of "going into all the world" to make disciples?

The Domino Effect

On the surface, the selections seemed to be quite casual, maybe even random. Andrew, a disciple of John the Baptist, ran into Jesus and began to follow Him. Andrew immediately went and got his brother, Peter. Then, like falling dominos, Peter introduced his business partners, James and John, to Jesus. They followed, too. Peter (or Andrew) brought his neighbor Philip to a meeting. After hearing Jesus, Philip also went and found his neighbor, Nathaniel.

I think about the Domino Effect in my own discipleship history. In Jackson, Mississippi, I attended the First Presbyterian youth group because it seemed like half my high school was going. I had so many invitations, I'm not exactly sure which one actually caused me to respond. I had to see what I was missing. My first week at Mississippi State University (MSU), I met Walter, who was planting a new church near the MSU campus. He invited me to the launch service. I invited my roommate, Greg, who eventually invited an MSU track athlete named Jerome. Months later, several of us invited Rice to church. Rice ministered to a football player named Curtis, who brought a half dozen of his teammates to our small church.

Many years later in Manila, Ferdie came to one of our first outreach meetings. I started discipling Ferdie our second week in the Philippines. A few years later, Ferdie started discipling a student named Rico, who brought his younger brother, Roy, to church, then his sister Noreena, then Jay, Ria, and Jolina, and then his mother. Eventually his dad, Johnny, started attending a discipleship group with businessmen, and responded to the Gospel. Around the same time, Rico's classmate, Vinay, came around. Then he brought to church his sister, Varsha, who then brought their mother.

This is how the Gospel works its way into family and friendship networks. Those who encounter Christ immediately invite friends, relatives, and classmates to "come and see." Following Christ does not mean abandoning friends and family. In fact, the most successful evangelism strategies focus on immediately equipping new believers to share their faith, to lead small-group Bible studies, and to include all their non-Christian friends.

In retrospect, we should come to realize that there's nothing random about the power of the Holy Spirit working in these networks. God, by His sovereign plan, puts people together, knowing that one life will affect the next like falling dominos.

Four Essentials of Effective Biblical Discipleship

The mission of Every Nation is the Great Commission, to make disciples of all nations. For me, that has never been about massive church buildings, mega-congregations, high-tech equipment, media events, celebrity members, or anything else. Every Nation in Yangoon, Myanmar, doesn't have much of a building, but they are world-class at making disciples. Compared to churches in the West, Every Nation Katmandu in Nepal, isn't very high-tech, but they're better than most at making disciples. Every Nation in Fusagasuga, Columbia, has sub-par musical instruments, but that doesn't hinder them from making disciples.

Every Nation is first and foremost about making disciples, and we're committed to following that strategy wherever it leads us. If it means our churches are large or small, influential or obscure, popular or persecuted — making disciples is the mission. It is Plan A; we have no Plan B.

Ministry leaders always talk about making disciples. After all, what leader is going to stand up and proclaim, "I don't believe in making disciples"? Discipleship is so ingrained in the ministry of Jesus and church history, no one can get away from it. At the very least, church leaders have to pay lip service to discipleship, even if there's very little in the way of actual discipleship going on. In other words, not all discipleship efforts and programs are equally effective. Just because people faithfully attend meetings, doesn't necessarily mean they are being discipled. Even if we lead or attend a weekly small-group Bible study at Starbucks, it doesn't necessarily mean we're effectively making disciples.

Four essential components make up an effective discipleship process. Those components are "essential" because if we skip, exclude, or can't figure out how to implement any one of those components, our effectiveness will diminish correspondingly. Here are the big four with brief explanations:

1. **Engaging Culture and Community.** When Jesus told His disciples to go and make disciples of all the nations, none of them thought He meant for them to gather people who already believed and start little discipleship groups. That's certainly not what He intended and certainly not what they did. By "make disciples," the implication is that we start from scratch. The discipleship process starts when we engage our culture and communities with the goal of introducing nonbelievers to the Gospel and to the Person of Jesus Christ.

   In chapter 11, I talked about the Ninety-Nine-and-the-One strategy found in Jesus's parable of a shepherd looking for a single lost sheep. This approach to ministry assumes that somehow, and in some way, everyone engages their community for Christ. On a college campus, that might mean joining campus organizations and inviting students to a dorm Bible study. In a community setting, it could mean coaching a neighborhood youth soccer team, volunteering at social service agencies, mentoring in the schools, or starting a small group Bible study and inviting non-believers. We're under no illusion that we can make disciples of the nations, our neighborhoods, or our friends without consistently engaging nonbelievers.

2. **Establishing Biblical Foundations.** To effectively make disciples, we have to be intentional about establishing foundations. It's written in the Gospels:

   > Why do you call me, "Lord, Lord," and do not do what I say? As for everyone who comes to me and hears my words and puts them into practice, I will show you what they are like. They are like a man building a house, who dug down deep and laid the foundation on rock. When a flood came, the

torrent struck that house but could not shake it, because it was well built" (Luke 6:46–48).

The passage above is used all the time to emphasize the importance of teaching and learning fundamental elements of authentic Christianity — the doctrinal underpinnings of our faith such as the incarnation, justification by faith, the atonement, the nature and character of God, and so on. I recognize the importance of these biblical concepts and what can happen if believers aren't clear about what they believe. I also understand that there's a difference in knowing the truth about Jesus, believing the truth about Jesus, and actually following Jesus. We can know and believe all the right stuff but still not be His disciple.

That was precisely the point of Jesus's illustration. The two houses in the storm represented two kinds of people, both hearers of Jesus's words. Whether or not one's spiritual foundations were deeply dug and founded on a rock was not about teaching and learning. A strong, enduring foundation was the result of *putting the Lord's words into practice*, not simply knowing the Word. If we want to help believers develop strong foundations, the thrust of our impartation should be focused on helping them practice Jesus' words, not just to understand or to confess them. If we want to prepare believers to withstand the storms of life, then we must teach them to consistently act on the Lord's command and to personally experience His promises.

It's not enough to merely teach about the preeminence of Christ; we must also challenge young believers to practice repentance and live a life of daily submission to His Lordship in all areas of life. It's not enough to simply teach the doctrine of the Holy Spirit; we must lay our hands on them and pray for them to be baptized in the Spirit. It's not enough to teach about the authority of Scripture and the power of prayer; we must help them cultivate the habits of daily prayer and Bible reading. It's not enough to teach them that God so loved the world; we must also equip and empower them to go and make disciples of all nations.

3. **Equipping Disciples to Minister.** This same Paul who started ministering to others as soon as he had his life-changing encounter with Jesus, wrote about the secret of spiritual maturity in his letter to the Ephesians:

> It was he [Jesus] who gave some to be apostles, some to be prophets, some to be evangelists, and some to be pastors and teachers, to prepare God's people for works of service, so that the body of Christ may be built up until we all reach unity in the faith and in the knowledge of the Son of God and become mature, attaining to the whole measure of the fullness of Christ. (Ephesians 4:11–14)

In verse 11, Paul identified the mentors as apostles, prophets, evangelists, pastors, and teachers. In verse 12, he gave their job description: "to prepare God's people for works of service." The King James Version translates that job description as "equipping God's people for the work of the ministry." The practical application of this passage is for professional, full-time pastors, teachers, and church staff to understand that their primary role is to serve as mentors to people. Their job is not to *do* all the ministry, but to *equip* all the people to do ministry.

For this discipleship concept to work its way through an entire organization, it has to be the prevailing culture from top to bottom. Senior leaders are the key. We cannot create an effective discipleship culture if senior leaders are primarily ministers rather than primarily equippers. And we can't create an effective discipleship culture if church members have a spectator mentality.

4. **Empowering Disciples to Make Disciples.** While in seminary, I had many talented, dedicated, and intelligent classmates who ended up doing nothing with their ministry training because they were in churches that didn't empower them to do ministry. Because of the lack of opportunity, some of them pioneered new churches and ministries with varying results. What's the point of equipping if we don't empower? If there's no direction, encouragement, or mechanism for empowering those we equip, then discipleship is a

dead-end street. For discipleship to be effective, we must make sure that engaging, establishing, and equipping comes full-circle. We do that by empowering disciples to make disciples.

There are many ways to implement all the components of an effective discipleship process. Every culture and every community will require a unique application. To be truly effective in making disciples, the church in each community has to figure out its own way of making all four discipleship components work together.

Why So Many Are Ineffective
The reason discipleship in so many churches is not as effective as it could be, is that there are myths about the discipleship process surrounding each essential component.

- **The Myth About Isolation.** The myth is that if we want to have an effective discipleship process, we need to separate new believers from their old friends. Back in our college days, Rice Broocks used to talk about the "Christian ghetto," meaning the places where Christian students hung out to isolate themselves from the real world that included "sinners" on campus. Following Jesus doesn't mean that we cut off all contact with our non-religious friends so we don't catch what they have. Rather, we need to engage them so that they catch what we have.

    Christianity spreads a lot like an airborne virus. That's especially true on university campuses, where large numbers of people live in close proximity to one another and interact on a regular basis. It's also true in any friendship network. Because each newly infected person becomes a carrier, hanging around friends has the potential to start a full-scale Gospel epidemic. Each time another person is affected by a carrier, the potential impact of the Gospel multiplies exponentially. Standard procedure to defeat the spread of such an epidemic is to quarantine infected individuals until the contagion stage is over. The important part is that new believers don't go into isolation but share their story with everyone with whom they come in contact. An effective discipleship program quickly equips new believers with the simple Gospel and immediately empowers them to evangelize their friends as soon as possible — while they're still highly contagious.

- **The Myth About Teaching Foundations.** The Great Commission mandates that we make disciples of all nations. Matthew 28:20 explains how we are to make disciples: "teaching them to obey everything I have commanded you." The myth is that establishing a solid foundation is only about knowing the doctrine. Effective discipleship not only teaches the truth but also enables new believers to experience the reality of it. It's not just teaching, but teaching them to live it. The Gospel of Luke says,

  > But the one who hears my words *and does not put them into practice* is like a man who built a house on the ground without a foundation. The moment the torrent struck that house, it collapsed and its destruction was complete. (Luke 6:49)

- **The Myth About Maturity.** My pastor's job is not primarily to minister to me, but to equip me to minister to others. Even if I don't pray enough, even if I'm not mature enough, even if I don't know enough Bible verses, even if I have too many past sins, even if I'm too young, even if I lost my temper yesterday — God is ready to use me now, though I may not feel qualified. The myth is that I must be a mature Christian before I step out to minister to others. The truth is that no one will mature unless they first step out in faith to minister to others.

- **The Myth About Ministry.** In November 2008, I was speaking at a leadership conference in Singapore to about 120 of Every Nation's Asian pastors, missionaries, and church planters. Some were from China; others were pioneering churches in Iran, Mongolia, Vietnam, and Bangladesh. Many had experienced intense persecution. Others were expecting it soon. Not an ounce of laziness or apathy could be found in that room. I knew that these young men and women were all aggressive, hardworking, high-commitment people who were willing and ready to do anything for the sake of the Gospel. My opening comment to them was, "If you're not experiencing the kind of fruitfulness you desire, it's not because you're too lazy to minister. Quite the contrary, it might be because you minister too much." Continuing the thought, I asked, "Do you spend more time ministering to people or preparing people to minister?" The myth about ministry is this: the more *I* minister to others, the more effective *I* will be at making disciples. Actually, the opposite is true. Ministering too much will cause your discipleship efforts to be ineffective and will prevent churches from growing and multiplying. Why? Because discipleship and growth happen when leaders empower others to minister. Sometimes the best approach is to get out of the way so that others can do the ministry. They may make mistakes, but I can live with that. I make plenty of mistakes. So do you.

The Hundred-Year Question

All four of those myths together comprise common, but unbiblical thinking in many churches. No wonder discipleship programs are less effective than they could be. It doesn't matter how many official church members we have or how many visitors attended our Easter services. What matters is how many of our members are making disciples and how many of our visitors are being discipled. Jesus taught, healed, and fed the crowds, but His prime time was given to His disciples. They were the ones who would reproduce themselves millions of times over. Making disciples is our only plan.

Everyone knows that last words are important. Jesus' last words to His disciples were simple: "Go and make disciples of all nations." His last words must be our first priority. What will happen to Every Nation in the next one hundred years if we fail to pass the disciple-making baton to the next generation? What could Every Nation become in the next one hundred years if we take those last words of Jesus seriously and make discipleship our top priority?

THIRTEEN

INVISIBLE LEADERS

A leader is best when people barely know he exists,
when his work is done, his aim fulfilled, they will say:
we did it ourselves.

— Lao Tzu (600 BC)

Whoever wants to become great among you must
become the servant of all.

— Jesus (Mark 9:35)

"HEY DAD, WHOSE CHURCH IS BIGGER, Nathan's, Stephen's, or ours?"

My middle son was in fourth grade at the time. His friends, Nathan and Stephen, are both sons of American missionary church-planters in the Philippines.

"That's a strange question, James. Why do you want to know?" Back then, my sons, like most of my staff, were clueless about the attendance of our church. It's just not something we talk about or celebrate. And we certainly don't compare our number to others.

"During lunch today, Nathan and Stephen were arguing about whose church is bigger, and I was just wondering if we're bigger than them."

"What did you say while they were arguing about their churches?"

"Nothing. I just sat there because I didn't know if we're bigger. Are we?"

"Both of those are huge churches."

"But what about our church? Are we bigger than them?" My sons are competitive about everything. Being biggest, fastest, strongest, and smartest is really important to them. Probably got it from their mother. It was obvious he was not letting this go, so I answered, "Well, if you're talking about Victory-Ortigas, then Stephen's church is bigger." At the time, Victory was one church in seven locations, and I was leading the Ortigas congregation in the Galleria Mall.

"But what if we're all in one place like at our conferences, and we add all the Victory people from the U-Belt, Alabang, Makati, Quezon City, and all the others. Would we be the biggest then?"

"Yep, if we add up all the Victory people all over Manila, we would be bigger."

"Would we be lots bigger?" To competitive young boys, being bigger is not enough when you can be *lots* bigger, just as winning a tennis match in split sets pales in comparison to winning in straight sets.

I refused to answer that last question, so he headed toward the door, then suddenly stopped, turned around, and asked one more question. This one was rhetorical, like he was thinking out loud to himself.

"Dad, but if we only met in one place, what would Pastor Luther do, and what would Pastor Joey do, and what would Pastor Manny do, and what would Pastor Ariel do?"

From the mouth of babes indeed!

My ten-year-old son seemed to understand what many mega-church pastors miss — that the job of the pastor is to equip and empower multiple generations of leaders and then get out of the way so they can lead. But if ministry is centered around a mega-leader, then others never get a chance to lead.

The hundred-year question forces us to think seriously about leadership development. If we want to be around in a hundred years, we better get serious about equipping and empowering multiple generations of leaders.

Heroic Leadership

In 1540, ten men with no money and no experience, but with a big vision, set out to change the world. They instinctively knew that their task would require them to develop leaders. So they focused on developing leaders and doing it quickly. Within a decade, despite their lack of experience in higher education, they had established over thirty colleges in Europe. By the end of the 1700s, they had over seven hundred schools on five continents.

Today the Jesuits are the world's largest religious order, including over two thousand institutions, in over a hundred nations, run by an army of over twenty-one thousand highly committed lifers, including Pope Francis. I don't agree with every point of their theology, but after decades of experience working with graduates of Jesuit institutions in the Philippines, I can say that they're still doing an excellent job of developing leaders. I've hired and worked with graduates from public schools, Protestant schools, and random Catholic schools, but the Jesuit institutions in the Philippines seem to crank out a higher ratio of leaders than their educational competitors.

Former Jesuit priest, Chris Lowney, in his book *Heroic Leadership*, summarized the Jesuit leadership development philosophy:

The Jesuit approach examines leadership through a very different prism, and refracted through that prism, leadership emerges in a very different light. Four differences stand out:

- We're all leaders, and we're all leading all the time, well or poorly.

- Leadership springs from within. It's about who I am as much as what I do.

- Leadership is not an act. It is my life, a way of living.

- I never complete the task of becoming a leader. It's an ongoing process.

All churches, whether Catholic, Protestant, or Pentecostal, could learn a thing or two about leadership from the Jesuit founder, Ignatius Loyola, and his myriad followers. The four foundational leadership lessons above would be a good starting point.

For as long as I can remember, when pastors visit our church, they typically ask three questions: How do you get so many men involved in worship and discipleship? How do you have so many young people? Where do you get all those leaders? I only discovered *Heroic Leadership* a few years ago, but somehow I inadvertently or instinctively followed Lowney's version of the Jesuit leadership development philosophy from the beginning.

Solving the Leadership Shortage

A few years ago, a missionary in Manila familiar with our church repeatedly asked me where I found so many young Filipino leaders. I gave him the same response every time: "You don't really want to know."

"No, really. You have to tell me. Where did you find so many strong young Filipino leaders?" My friend desperately needed to solve the leadership problem in his rapidly growing church.

"Believe me, they didn't look like this when I found them. It took hard work and a long time to get them to this level of leadership." In other words, sorry to disappoint you with the truth, but leadership development is a long, arduous process, not a magical altar-call moment.

After one of these conversations, my impatient friend asked me if he could hire some of our leaders since we had so many. I told him to make his best offer. No matter how much money was offered, I didn't expect any of our leaders to jump ship. The moral of the story: sons and daughters are born, not bought. But birthing leaders is only the start; the next step is to develop them.

Several years ago, after a decade of explosive church growth, our leadership development was not keeping pace with our evangelism, causing serious leadership shortages at all levels of the organization. We needed more small group leaders, more ushers, more worship leaders, more kids ministry volunteers, more lead pastors, more campus missionaries, more executive assistants — we needed them all, and we needed them yesterday.

To solve our leadership shortage, we gathered with about thirty leaders for three days of emergency soul-searching, problem solving, and brainstorming. Much of the time was spent picking my brain and Deborah's brain about how we developed so many leaders back in the day. We honestly didn't know what we did or why we had so many great leaders. But whatever we did to discover, develop, equip, and empower potential leaders had carried us, until recently when our growth zoomed past our leadership development structure like it was standing still. Through hours of thorough questions, desperate prayers, and wise discussions, we came up with four essential parts to develop an empowering leadership culture. We called our discovery *iLead.* Here are the four pillars of leadership development we unearthed that week:

1. **Identification.** The goal in this first phase of leadership development is to help a person identify their calling, gifts, and opportunities. Everyone is called, everyone is gifted, and everyone has opportunities to minister and lead. But few understand calling, fewer develop gifts, and hardly anyone walks through open doors. I only realized I was called to be a cross-cultural church planter after I walked through the open door that was a summer mission trip to Manila's University Belt. Had I not recognized and entered that open door, I don't think I would have ever understood my calling or developed my gifts. Identification is also about a leader identifying potential leaders to include in the iLead leadership-development process.

2. **Instruction.** Two seminary classes have continued to shape my life and ministry for decades. How I do church and mission was transformed by a Cross-Cultural Hermeneutics class taught by Dr. Larry Caldwell at Asian Theological Seminary (ATS). And how I read, study, interpret, and preach the Bible was shaped by a class on the book of Genesis taught by Dr. Nomer Bernardino, also at ATS. We all benefit from instruction. It's part of the Great Commission. In order to make disciples of all nations, we must teach them to observe everything Jesus taught. Instruction can be face-to-face or from a distance via podcast, e-mail, Skype (we call that "diskypleship"), books, TV, radio, or the Internet. Paul instructed Timothy from a distance saying, "Although I hope to come to you soon, I am writing you these instructions so that if I am delayed, you will know how people ought to conduct themselves in God's

household" (1 Timothy 3:14–15). Whether face-to-face or from a distance, the goal of instruction is transformation, not just transference of information.

3. **Impartation.** While instruction can be done from a remote location via letters or Skype, impartation seems to require close proximity. My friend, Ralph Moore, one of the most prolific disciple-makers, leadership developers, and church planters alive today, says that "Disciple making invades personal space." Consider Paul's letter to the Romans, whom he had never met face-to-face: "I long to see you so that I may impart to you some spiritual gift to make you strong" (Romans 1:11). Paul could instruct them from afar, but that wasn't enough. He felt the need to get face-to-face and to "invade their personal space." Impartation transfers spiritual gifts and makes us strong. I'm not an evangelist, but every time I get around Rice Broocks, I want to preach the Gospel to a skeptic. I am strengthened and get a small dose of the evangelistic gift. That's impartation. That's why the laying on of hands is a foundational teaching of the church (Hebrews 6:1–2).

4. **Internship.** On-the-job training seemed to be the primary method of leadership development in the New Testament church. Identification, instruction, and impartation are vital, but the greatest learning comes from actually doing ministry. As a new believer, Paul traveled with Barnabas as an intern. Many years later, Paul employed the same development strategy, taking along Timothy as his intern. Of course, Jesus handpicked twelve young men to be part of His internship program. Along the way, Jesus helped them identify callings, gifts, and opportunities. He also gave them divine instruction. But the ultimate leadership development was being His intern. Internship has three parts: observation, participation, and evaluation. Observation means we watch while the leader leads. Participation means we lead with the leader. Evaluation means the leader watches as we lead.

The Hubris Born of Success

As I watch young leaders preach better sermons, build bigger buildings, and lead more influential churches than anyone in my generation, I rejoice and tremble. I rejoice because, like the apostle John, "I have no greater joy than to hear that my children are walking in the truth" (3 John 1:4). I tremble because I know that success and influence are more dangerous to a leader than failure and obscurity.

How the Mighty Fall by Jim Collins is probably the scariest book I have ever read. The scariest part of the book was what Collins identified as the beginning of the end of great companies — the "Hubris Born of Success."

The Bible says it like this: "Pride goes before destruction, a haughty spirit before a fall" (Proverbs 16:18).

While Collins wrote to business leaders about business failures, the principles of success and failure equally apply to churches and church leaders.

In one case study, Collins explained how Motorola's explosive growth in the mid-1990s from $5 billion to $27 billion in annual revenues "contributed to a cultural shift from humility to arrogance." As quick as arrogance replaced humility, Motorola's "cutting edge" analog cell phones were left in the dust by their digital competition. Why didn't the Motorola big-shots see the digital revolution coming? Because they were blinded by the "Hubris Born of Success." Many pastors and churches are likewise impressed with, and blinded by, their own success and are teetering on the edge of a dangerous cliff, about to fall. The only remedy is humility, acknowledging that all success is from God, for God, and in spite of us.

Later in the book, Collins described the leaders who successfully navigated their companies through the dangerous waters of success. He writes:

> The best leaders we've studied had a peculiar genius for seeing themselves as not all that important, recognizing the need to build an executive team and to craft a culture based on core values that do not depend upon a single heroic leader. But in cases

of decline, we find a more pronounced role for the powerful individual, and not for the better.

Invisible Leaders

Since he was already dead, I don't think D. L. Moody actually read *How the Mighty Fall*, but he passionately warned leaders about the "Hubris Born of Success."

Pointing to the Gospel writers as examples of humility, Moody warned leaders to stay invisible.

> Matthew takes up his pen to write, and he keeps Matthew out of sight. He tells what Andrew and Peter did; but he calls himself Matthew the publican. He tells how they left all to follow Christ, but he does not mention the feast *he* gave.

Moody points out that Mark, who wrote his Gospel under the authority of Peter, describes some of the most embarrassing moments of Peter's life, and Peter did not edit those stories out. Of Luke, he says, "You cannot find Luke's name; he keeps out of sight. He wrote two books, and his name is not to be found in either."

Moody's humility warning ends with this exhortation to spiritual leaders: "Dear man of God, I would that I had the same spirit that I could *just get out of sight — hide myself.*"

Nelson Mandela described the invisible leader: "It is better to lead from behind and to put others in front, especially when you celebrate victory when nice things occur. You take the front line when there is danger. Then people will appreciate your leadership."

The Hundred-Year Question

Will Every Nation even exist in one hundred years if we do not make leadership development a priority? What will Every Nation look like in one hundred years if we stay committed to leadership development, if we make equipping and empowering the next generation an intentional priority, and if we stay humble and resist the "Hubris Born of Success"?

FOURTEEN

SUCCESSFUL FAILURES

A man who doesn't spend time with his family can never be a real man.

— Vito Corleone, *The Godfather*

By faith Noah, when warned about things not yet seen, in holy fear built an ark to save his family.

— Hebrews 11:7

I WOKE UP EARLY this morning. Jet lag makes me feel real spiritual, at least for a few days. While I sat sipping hot Earl Grey tea, reading my Bible, and enjoying the sunrise from what used to be my son's bedroom in our Manila apartment, Deborah walked in, hugged me, and pointed to the clock. "It's 6:18, April 5. William was born twenty-seven years ago. Remember fighting in Makati Med over who would hold him first?"

One of our best fights ever. I remember that day like it was yesterday.

Twenty-seven years ago. Wow! (Technically it's still the fourth where he is in Nashville, but since he was born in Manila, we're already celebrating.)

I serendipitously ran into one of William's baseball coaches a couple of days ago. Hadn't seen him in years. We chatted briefly about our sons. My mind was flooded with good memories the rest of the day.

Twenty-seven years ago. Really?

Every parent knows that the birth of the first child marks the end of life as we know it. Marriage *changed* my life, but the birth of our first child *ended* the life I lived up to that moment and gave me a new one. A better one. A life filled with adventure. And joy. And a lot of other stuff.

William was born five weeks after a revolution in the Philippines that ousted the president, Ferdinand Marcos. In that third week of February 1986, it seemed that all Americans, except us, were fleeing the country. We stayed because there was no way the airlines would allow a passenger as pregnant as Deborah on a plane. We had no money to purchase a ticket anyway. Those were exciting times to be in Manila.

Twenty-seven years ago. Can he really be that old?

Looking back, Deborah and I made one decision that we'll never regret. We certainly made plenty of decisions we regret, but we got the big one right. Here it is: We decided that family would be first. Not ministry. Family. We decided that we would do family and ministry in such a way that our kids would always know that they are more important to us than ministry. Here's a sad story that helped us make that decision.

I Don't Pray Enough

Deborah and I had been in Manila a few years, wondering how to lead a church that would impact this sprawling city of millions. I heard that a huge church was hosting a church-growth conference in a neighboring nation that promised answers. I signed up, along with a couple of young Filipino campus ministers.

At the conference, we were part of a group of seven hundred pastors from twenty-five nations, all ready to learn how to grow a big strong church. Before me stood a man I had respected and admired for years. His books were international bestsellers. His unique church and his passionate preaching inspired millions around the world. His prayer life was exemplary, his ministry legendary. And his accent was thick, which only added to his mystique.

Our goal was to learn the principles that had enabled him to be what many considered "the most successful pastor in the world." In the first session, he told us there were three keys to his phenomenal success: the power of prayer, the presence of the Holy Spirit, and visionary goal-setting.

"Pray and obey," he repeated over and over. But when he said pray, he meant four to six hours a day! I now officially felt like a failure. This dude wakes up at four every morning and prays until six. Then he eats breakfast and prays some more. Then he eats lunch and prays some more. As I listened to this Asian praying machine, I accepted that I would probably never lead a large church, because there was no way I could pray six hours every day.

He continued, "When you pray and obey [i.e., four to six hours a day] you invite the presence of the Holy Spirit to do miracles in your ministry." *I guess my anemic prayer life explains the lack of Holy Spirit miracle power in my ministry.*

Then he got to the visionary goal-setting part of his speech. He said, "Everything starts with visions and dreams. Before you give birth to a child, you must first become pregnant. Before your prayers give birth, you must be pregnant with vision. Goals and visions and dreams are very, very important. When people do not set goals, they do not believe."

I'm not a goal-setter. Never have been. Never will be. In fact, I'm allergic to goals. So at this point in the seminar, I felt my best move would be to resign and look for a real job back in the States. Then he said something that rocked my world.

A Humble Confession of Failure

Halfway through his second session, he made a statement that's permanently etched on my heart. I'm sure I'll never forget it; at least, I hope I won't. I pray you won't either. Here's that unforgettable, life-changing, shocking quote from the world's most successful pastor:

"I have failed as a father."

He prefaced that confession with this statement. "I am often asked how to balance family and ministry. I do not know. I have failed as a father."

My heart broke as the words rolled off his tongue. With deep regret and with his heavy signature accent, he made his humble confession. The words echoed in my mind like a shout in an empty cave, "I have failed as a father . . . failed as a father . . . failed as a father . . . "

He dropped his head as he said it. I dropped my head, too. I silently prayed for his three adult sons. I prayed for the other seven hundred pastors and church leaders at the conference. "May we not follow in his footsteps, at least not in this area." I also prayed for my three young sons. "Oh God, don't let me be so busy winning the world that I lose my sons! Don't let me fail them."

As I silently prayed, this man continued his sobering story. He informed us that he had recently taken his first family vacation in thirty-five years of ministry. It was during this vacation that his sons told him that they didn't "have any good memories" growing up as kids. Because he was so busy "serving God," he just didn't have time for his family. After sharing that with us, he said, "That really hurts my heart." I could tell it did. It hurt mine too.

Here was a man respected all over the world, author of numerous best-selling books, a famous preacher, and pastor of one of the most influential churches in the world. For thirty-five years, he had sacrificially given himself to his church, but not to his family. He had built a massive church, but he had failed to build his home. By his own admission, he was a success at church, but a failure at home.

I hope no one misunderstands me. My point here is not to criticize a great man of faith. My point is to build up the family. I still read this man's books on prayer and leadership. I'm still inspired by his faith and vision. Unlike many successful leaders, he seems to have realized his priorities were amiss, and he's trying to make amends.

True Success and True Sacrifice
That "failed as a father" statement caused me to reconsider what true success really looks like. Is it possible to be a good preacher and a bad parent? Is it possible to be a success at work and a failure at home?

Speaking about church leaders, Paul told Timothy, "He must manage his own family well. . . . If anyone does not know how to manage his own family, how can he take care of God's church?" (1 Timothy 3:4–5).

How should we determine if a person is qualified to be a pastor? Too often, it's based on educational achievements, oratory skills, and administrative abilities. The Bible says we should examine a man's family. Not his family tree, but his relationship with his wife and children. If this area is in order, then he might qualify to lead a church.

Too many pastors, missionaries, and church planters see their wives and children as distractions and hindrances to their ministries. A more biblical perspective is that a spiritual leader's home life either validates or repudiates the message preached.

A few months into my first year in the Philippines, in my never-ending quest to figure out how to impact a city of millions, I attempted to make an appointment with the pastors of the five largest churches in Manila. Only two agreed to meet with the new kid on the block. I'll never forget my interview with the pastor of a dynamic eight thousand-member mega-church.

Notebook and pen ready, I asked this veteran missionary how his church reached so many Filipinos. He soberly looked me in the eye and asked, "Are you sure you want a big church? There's a great price to pay." Already on the edge of my chair, I leaned forward and said I was ready and willing to make any sacrifice and pay any price to do what God had called me to do in Manila.

He continued, "Leading this church has cost me my family." Sadness was in his eyes and voice as he told me his story, admitting that his children wanted nothing to do with the church or ministry. This meeting happened a couple of years before the "failed as a father" confession already mentioned. Deborah and I didn't have children yet, but I walked out of this man's office vowing not to do church this way. My mind was racing. *There has to be a way to reach this city and not destroy my family in the process. God, you have to show me a better way to do this.*

Not long after this eye-opening, discouraging encounter, I was reading Hebrews. God seemed to speak loud and clear when I got to the part about Noah in chapter 11: "By faith Noah, when warned about things not yet seen, in holy fear built an ark to save his family" (Hebrews 11:7).

Consider the Genesis account of that same story: "The Lord then said to Noah, "Go into the ark, you *and your whole family*" (Genesis 7:1).

Noah's response to God's call to build the ark saved his family. God expected Noah to get on the ark along with his family, not to leave his family behind.

Am I saying there aren't sacrifices in ministry? No. Whether we're called to a grass hut or a glass tower, the call of God always involves sacrifice. But we're not called to sacrifice family for ministry. Noah sacrificed much to obey, God's call. His sacrificial obedience saved his family and the world. Too many leaders today lose their family in the process of saving the world. It shouldn't be that way.

Do you want to save the world? Saving your family is step one.

It's About Priorities, Not Perfection

Lest anyone misunderstand me, let me be clear that I am not saying that leaders must have perfect families. What I am saying is that leaders must have proper priorities.

Consider Samuel, the prophet, and his spiritual mentor Eli, the priest. Both leaders raised evil sons. Eli was judged because of his family. Samuel was not. Why?

Eli did a great job mentoring Samuel, but failed to mentor his own sons. Here's how the Bible describes them: "Eli's sons were scoundrels; they had no regard for the Lord. . . . This sin of the young men was very great in the Lord's sight, for they were treating the Lord's offering with contempt" (1 Samuel 2:12, 17).

Though Samuel was one of the most godly men in the Bible, his sons were no better than Eli's. "But his sons did not follow his ways. They turned aside after dishonest gain and accepted bribes and perverted justice" (1 Samuel 8:3).

So, why did Eli's worthless sons seemingly destroy his ministry while Samuel's equally worthless sons did not disqualify him? This verse gives us a clue: "For I told him [Eli] that I would judge his family forever *because of the sin he knew about*; his sons blasphemed God, and *he failed to restrain them*" (1 Samuel 3:13).

Actually, Eli wasn't judged because of the wickedness of his adult sons. He was judged because *he* knew about their sin and *he* did nothing about it. He stuck his head in the sand and went about ministry business as usual. He allowed his sinful sons to continue as spiritual leaders, knowing they were disqualified.

The leadership lesson is obvious. If there's a problem at home, admit it and do something about it. Get help where needed. But don't pretend nothing's wrong and hope that no one notices.

Again, it's about priorities, not perfection. My family isn't perfect, but family is my top priority.

The Hundred-Year Question

If there is ever a sphere that we must think long-term about, it is the family. How we do family absolutely impacts generation after generation. What will Every Nation become in one hundred years if we sacrifice our families on the altar of ministry and financial success? On the other hand, what will Every Nation look like in one hundred years if we prioritize our families while pursuing our mission?

CULTURE

- *Vision*
- *Generosity*
- *Diversity*
- *Sacrifice*

FIFTEEN

THE SMOKE
OF A THOUSAND VILLAGES

*Vision: the act or power of anticipating that which will
or may come to be.*

*I have seen, at different times, the smoke of a thousand
villages — villages whose people are without Christ,
without God, and without hope in this world.*
— Robert Moffat (1795–1883)

Where there is no vision, the people perish.
— Proverbs 29:18 (KJV)

PRIOR TO THE UNITED STATE'S ENTRY into World War II, Robert
Woodruff, then president of Coca-Cola, announced his vision: "We
will see that every man in uniform gets a bottle of Coke for five cents,
wherever he is in the world and no matter how much it costs us." His
post-war cola vision was even more ambitious. He dreamed of the day
when "everyone in the world would have an opportunity to taste a
Coke."

Woodruff captured three essential elements of vision that we must
embrace if we're to establish churches and campus ministries in every
nation.

Coca-Cola and the Cost of Vision

First of all, the Coke vision was a world vision. It wasn't enough to sell
Coke at every baseball stadium in America and every hockey rink in

Canada. So what if Coke was selling more than all its soft drink competitors combined? Woodruff would not rest until Coke was in every nation. In the same way, God has entrusted us with a world vision. It's not enough to build a mega-church that reaches one city. It's not enough if our church is bigger than the church down the road. Our vision must reach at least as far as Coke's.

The second vision lesson from Coke is the value of individual people. Mr. Woodruff's vision for Coke grew in time to include, not just every place in the world, but every person in the world. Growth is the nature of vision. If our vision only includes people like us, then it's too small and we need a bigger dream. I don't know if Coke is actually available to every person on the planet yet, but they must be close. What a tragedy it would be if every person gets a taste of Coke before they get a taste of the Living Water. Yes, we have a vision to reach every nation, but it can't stop there. We must also have a vision to reach every person in every nation with the Gospel.

Finally, Woodruff realized there was a cost involved in taking Coke to every man in uniform anywhere in the world, and he was not intimidated by that cost. He was determined that all American soldiers would have a drink of Coke if they wanted one. He was willing to swallow the cost as long as those men in uniform could swallow a Coke.

Every time Jesus spelled out the vision and destiny He had for His disciples, He added that there was a cost. They would be required to carry a cross, to deny self, to forsake all, to follow Him. Make no mistake about it, there's a cost in having a world vision. But no matter the cost, we must be at least as dedicated to Christ's vision as the president of Coke was to his.

Because Jesus died for the whole world, we can never be content just being a local church doing local ministry. We must pay the price to reach every person in every nation in our generation.

From Cape Town to Cairo, and Everywhere Else

Several years ago, I had the honor of meeting a legendary and visionary German evangelist named Reinhard Bonnke. In the past decade, Bonnke and his team have recorded over fifty-two million documented decisions for Christ through massive open-air Gospel meetings, primarily in Africa. That was not a typo. Read it again. Fifty. Two. Million. Bonnke's evangelism and healing meetings have accommodated up to 1.6 million people in a single service. That's a lot of people. I hate to admit it, but I never think that big.

In my mind, this guy was a larger-than-life, iconic super-hero of the Faith. In reality, he was just an old man with a thick German accent and worn-out knees who still burns with a contagious vision to preach the Gospel from "Cape Town to Cairo" and everywhere else on the planet. I want to be like him when I grow up — not an evangelist, but a man who dreams big dreams and has the same passion at the finish line that he had at the starting line.

Bonnke and I were the guest speakers at the 2011 National Conference for Australian Christian Churches in Brisbane. When I heard that he was the other speaker, I wanted to give him my speaking slots so I could sit and listen and take notes from perhaps the greatest evangelist alive.

Before and after meetings, I got to hang out with Bonnke and his team in the green room. On stage he's like Superman: bold, strong, powerful, and loud. Face-to-face he's more like Clark Kent: humble, unassuming, gracious, and soft-spoken. And I found out he rides the same motorcycle that I ride. (We're both partial to German engineering.) Anyway, I don't think I have ever been around a man with such a unique balance of vision, passion, and humility. No matter what the topic, somehow, he always throws in his "from Cape Town to Cairo" vision that's been the driving force of his life and ministry for more than four decades. Cape Town to Cairo covers a whole continent. *Lord, help me pray, dream, and strategize in terms of continents, not just communities, campuses, and cities.*

When that "Cape Town to Cairo" vision first arrested him, he was a young German pastor on a short mission trip to Lesotho in southern Africa. On that trip, God burned into his heart a vision of "the continent of Africa, washed in the precious Blood of Jesus — an entire continent, from Cape Town to Cairo and from Dakar to Djibouti."

That vision seems to burn hotter the older Bonnke gets. Here's how he introduces himself in chapter one of his forty-chapter, 650-page autobiography, *Living a Life of Fire*:

> Hot tears seek the corners of my eyes. This is joy beyond any I have known. I smile and tilt my head up, looking into a sky of ancient constellations. I feel the Creator of the Universe smiling down on this corner of the world tonight. I breathe deeply. The smoke of cooking fires paints the breeze and brings me back to earth. I am a thousand miles from anywhere normal, and this is where I feel most at home. We have found another forgotten state where few have heard the way of salvation. I am Reinhard Bonnke, an evangelist. Welcome to my destiny.

Speaking about his calling and vision, Bonnke says,

> I eat it, I sleep it, I dream it, I speak it, I write it, I pray it, I weep it, I laugh it. It is my wish to die preaching this Gospel. I am like a starving man until I can stand again with a microphone in my hand, looking across a sea of faces, shouting the words of His love into the darkness.

After hanging around Reinhard Bonnke, I prayed that God would help me think bigger.

Learning How to Think Big

In order to help Abraham embrace a bigger vision for his life, God used three word-pictures to break him out of his limited mindset:

1. "I will make your offspring like the dust of the earth, so that if anyone could *count the dust*, then your offspring could be counted." (Genesis 13:16)

2. "He took him outside and said, 'Look up at the heavens and *count the stars* — if indeed you can count them.' Then he said to him, 'So shall your offspring be.'" (Genesis 15:5)

3. "I will surely bless you and make your descendants as numerous as the stars in the sky and as the sand on the seashore." (Genesis 22:17)

God picked three items that were way beyond Abraham's ability to count: dust, sand, and stars. That's thinking big!

At Victory Weekend retreats in the Philippines, Ferdie Cabiling has often used a Mr. Miyagi trick to help people think big. Ferdie would take new believers outside at night and have them lie on their backs and look up. Then he would say, "Start counting." As they began to count stars, Ferdie would quote the verses about descendants as numerous as stars. Then he would quote and pray verses from the New Testament about fruitfulness. The night session ends when Ferdie says, "Now, get up, and go and make disciples."

I don't count dust, sand, or stars, or watch the smoke from cooking fires, but I do count nations. Every time I see a map or a flag, they remind me of our vision, and I start claiming Psalm 2:8, "Ask of me, and I will make the nations your inheritance, the ends of the earth your possession." What sand and stars did for Abraham, and flags and maps do for me, the smoke from cooking fires did for one of my heroes of the faith.

The Smoke of a Thousand Villages

On our first London visit many years ago, Deborah and I did the obligatory Westminster Abby tour where we visited the tombs of the most important people in England's history. The Abby is the final resting place of kings, queens, playwrights, poets, scientists, statesmen, and a missionary. It was that missionary's tomb that most interested me. His body was buried in London, but his heart was buried under a tree in southern Africa. True story.

David Livingstone was a Scottish medical missionary, pioneer, explorer, adventurer, and national hero. He was born in 1813, in Scotland, and died sixty years later in 1873 in what is now Zambia. His heart is still in Africa.

Livingstone believed that if he could establish "legitimate trade" and spread Christianity throughout Africa, then the slave trade could be destroyed. This dual vision to spread Christianity in Africa and end slavery consumed him until the day he died. That he became a national hero and famous celebrity was an accidental side note to his lifework.

To understand Livingstone's passion for his vision, we have to meet his father-in-law.

Robert Moffat arrived in Cape Town as a missionary in 1817. The driving force behind his lifework is summed up in his famous saying, "I have seen, at different times, the smoke of a thousand villages — villages whose people are without Christ, without God, and without hope in this world."

David Livingstone married Moffat's oldest daughter, and until the day he died, was also driven by Moffat's "smoke of a thousand villages" vision for Africa.

After a life of following the smoke signals all over Africa, on May 1, 1873, Livingstone was found dead on his knees in prayer in a small village southeast of Lake Bangweulu in present-day Zambia. He died from a lethal combination of malaria, dysentery, and internal bleeding. On the morning of his death, Livingstone's friends, Susi and Chuma, cut out his heart before his body was shipped to England for burial. His heart was then buried under a *mpundu* tree near the spot where he died on his knees. Today, the Livingstone Memorial sits on that spot covering Livingstone's heart.

Has your heart been captured by God's vision for your campus, your city, your country? Has your heart been captured by His vision for every nation?

The Vision Is for Runners, Not Websites

Twenty-six hundred years ago, God's people were being violently attacked by the ungodly Chaldeans. Those were dark times for Israel. People wondered why God would let this happen. They wondered about all the covenantal promises that God seemed to have forgotten. The prophet Habakkuk cried out to God and God answered:

> Write the vision
> And make it plain on tablets,
> That he may run who reads it.
> For the vision is yet for an appointed time;
> But at the end it will speak, and it will not lie.

Though it tarries, wait for it;
Because it will surely come. (Habakkuk 2:2–3)

I know there's a technical difference in dictionary definitions, but I tend to use the words *mission* and *vision* as synonyms. With that in mind, here's what we can learn about the mission/vision baton from Habakkuk.

- **Write the vision.** Vision must be written before it can be handed off. These pages are my best attempt at writing the Every Nation mission, vision, values, and culture.

- **Make it plain.** I have made no attempt to impress with obscure vocabulary or confuse with obtuse theology. No bells. No whistles. Just vision.

- **That he may run who reads it.** Vision is for runners, not for bulletin boards, bumper stickers, and web pages. It's my hope that thousands all over the world will run as fast as they can in every direction with the Every Nation baton and pass it to everyone who will receive it!

- **The vision is yet for an appointed time.** The Every Nation vision and mission is bigger than Every Nation's founders. There's no way it can be accomplished in our lifetime, but it will happen at its appointed time. It requires all of us to make disciples and to equip and empower multiple generations of leaders all over the world.

- **At the end it will speak, it will not lie.** Vision is not current reality, but it is still true. It does not lie. You've read some history and some stories on these pages, but you're also reading the vision we have for a great future. Visionaries are obsessed with the future, not stuck in the past.

- **Though it tarries, wait for it.** The bigger the vision, the longer it takes. So we need patience. We need to wait. Not a sit-around-doing-nothing kind of wait, but a work-hard-pray-harder kind of wait.

- **It will surely come.** If the vision is from God, it will happen. Maybe not as soon as we hope, but it will happen. Not because of our cleverness. Not because of our hard work. Not because of our slick marketing. It will happen because it's God's will.

The Hundred-Year Question

If you hang around with Every Nation people for very long, you'll quickly find that we're all a bit obsessed with vision, both local and global. Some churches only have local vision, others only have global vision, but we try to have both, all the time. It might feel like vision overload, but it's who we are. Vision is part of our culture. If you're not comfortable with vision, you probably won't be comfortable in an Every Nation church.

What will happen in Every Nation in one hundred years if we do not write the vision? What will happen if we do not run with the vision? What could happen in the next one hundred years if we faithfully write the vision that God has entrusted to us? What will happen if we passionately run with the vision to reach every nation?

SIXTEEN

IF I WERE A RICH MAN

Generosity: readiness or liberality in giving.

Earn all you can, give all you can, save all you can.
— John Wesley

It is more blessed to give than to receive.
— Jesus

MY YOUNGEST SON, JONATHAN, pinned an article on the bulletin board above his desk in his bedroom. He stuck it there his freshman year, and it stayed all four years he studied at Belmont University. It will probably be pinned on the bulletin board at his office for the next decade. Eventually, I asked him what was so special about that article that ranked it right up there next to the picture of Moriah (Jonathan's girlfriend at the time of the following conversation, fiancée at the time of this writing, and wife by the time you read this).

"The article was about some generous rich dude." Jonathan is not big on long explanations.

"Okay," I said. "Anything else?"

"He gave away lots of money."

Sometimes with sons, you have to press for details. "Right," I said. "Generous people tend to give. But what's so special about this William Borden guy?"

When I Get Rich

Surrendering to my interrogation, Jonathan explained, "I want to be super generous like this guy. One day, I hope my businesses will make millions, and I plan to give most of it away to help fight poverty in Africa. If I can't give away most of what I have when I don't have much, how will I be able to give away most when I have a lot? So I'm practicing giving now."

Too many of us are like Tevye in *Fiddler on the Roof*, dancing around singing, "If I were a rich man . . . dibby dibby dibby dum." And just like in Tevye's song, we'd probably spend our riches on ourselves, forgetting God until the last verse. Unlike the inner-Tevye in most of us, Jonathan had it backward, at least backward from the way most people think. So who was this William Borden guy, and how had he made such an impression on my son?

William Borden could be considered one of the greatest campus missionaries, or one of the greatest Christian givers, or one of the greatest Christian ministers ever. Take your pick. He was an extraordinary example of each.

William was born in 1887 into the significant wealth of a Chicago attorney (not heir to the Borden Dairy fortune as is sometimes attributed). He became a Christian at an early age and first felt the call to be a missionary while on a round-the-world tour before entering Yale University. Despite having experienced numerous spiritual awakenings since its founding in 1701, when Borden arrived on the campus in 1905, rationalism and skepticism had permeated Yale from top to bottom.

A group of incoming freshmen led by Borden began a network of prayer meetings that turned into a campus revival. As is often the case, the revival was met by opposition, and the primary opposition was from Yale professors. Nonetheless, by Borden's senior year, one thousand of the thirteen hundred students at Yale were meeting in small discipleship and prayer groups.

Borden and a few friends traveled to Nashville for the 1905 Student Volunteer Movement conference, held every fourth year. Dr. Samuel Zwemer, missionary to Egypt and expert on Islam, displayed a map that marked every mission station from China to West Africa, showing at the same time the vast areas with no Christian witness. Borden returned to Yale committed to being a missionary among the Muslims in Kansu, a remote region of China considered to be one of the most difficult mission assignments on earth.

While a student, he founded Yale Hope Mission in New Haven and was always at the Mission helping men who were "down on their luck." He was extraordinarily generous, but almost all of his giving was anonymous. Though he was, by inheritance, one of the wealthiest young men at Yale, few students knew it. Neither did they know that he was the source of numerous gifts, not only to Yale Hope Mission, but to other students. Borden was responsible for the "miraculous" provision of scholarship funds, enabling fellow students to attend the 1905 Student Volunteer Conference. He gave extremely generous gifts to missions, to the student movement, and even to retirement funds for missionaries. While still a student, Borden got involved with China Inland Mission, shouldering the financial burden for missionaries all over the world.

No Reserve, No Regrets
After graduating from Yale and then Princeton seminary, Borden spent three months speaking on over thirty campuses. According to the general secretary of the Student Volunteer Movement, the impact of Borden's dedication and testimony "were the most fruitful three months of the movement."

On December 12, 1912, Borden sailed for language school in Egypt. Within the first two weeks in Cairo, he had organized seminary students to distribute the *Khutbas* (a booklet by a converted Muslim) to the entire city of eight hundred thousand people. Within three months of his arrival, the young missionary contracted cerebral meningitis, and on April 15, at the age of twenty-five, William Borden slipped into eternity. His last words were scribbled on a piece of paper found under his pillow:

No reserve; no retreat; no regrets!

There was scarcely a US newspaper that did not publish a lengthy account of his short life. Memorial services were held all over the world, as well as at the Yale Hope Mission and the African Methodist Episcopal Church where Borden taught Sunday school while in seminary.

A biographical sketch of Borden's life for Muslim readers was published in five languages. Thirty-five thousand copies of the Chinese edition made their way into every province of China and even opened doors for mission stations in previously unreached areas. According to Dr. John R. Mott, the story of William Borden at the 1913 Student Volunteer Movement conference was the most powerful appeal for missionary service ever made by the SVM.

Borden inherited approximately $5 million and had given a good chunk of it away by the time he was twenty-five. In the fall of 1913, the wills of two extraordinary men were probated — William Borden and J.P. Morgan. Both were devout believers. Morgan was worth over $100 million; Borden was then worth about $1 million ($2 billion and $20 million in 2013 dollars). Yet, Borden's bequests to Christian causes almost doubled those of J.P. Morgan.

Who could have imagined William Borden's impact in such a short time — seven years as a student, six years as a philanthropist, and four months as a missionary? Yale Professor Charles Erdman summed up the opinion of many: "Apart from Christ, there is no explanation for such a life."

Predetermined Giving

Money and finances, tithing and capital campaigns, pew taxes and "mandatory love offerings" — have all been difficult (sometimes touchy) subjects throughout the entire history of the church. And something tells me that it's unlikely to get any easier in the next one hundred years. It may get harder; a whole lot harder.

How much, then, should we be giving?

Actually, that's the wrong question. Jesus talked more about why and in what spirit one gave, to the point that the amount was all but irrelevant. Remember the widow who felt compelled to put in her two cents.

One of my greatest encouragements is that, in so many ways and in so many areas, the next generation is leading the way — including the grace of giving. Jonathan's radical generosity has inspired and (I confess) worried me at times. I guess I'm like those disciples who questioned the wisdom of the woman who broke the alabaster vial and poured the ointment all over Jesus. Such extravagant giving! And it was her most valuable possession too. In fact, extravagant giving usually brings out questions and criticisms from those in the grandstands.

Several times during the months leading up to his wedding, I challenged Jonathan about his extravagant giving habits.

"Do you have plans to buy a house in the near future, or ever?"

"How are you going to send your kids to college?"

"Your budget works now, but what about when you get married?"

"Does Moriah understand what she's getting into when it comes to your view of giving?"

It was one of those conversations when a father injects himself into his son's private world because something just has to be said. With many other such parent-type questions, I was challenging Jonathan to give me his plan. Of course, I was expecting him to come back with something like, "I believe God will supply" (somehow), which was another way of saying, "Nope, got no plan at all."

What surprised me was that he had a very precise plan and had been working through the details for some time. He informed me that he had "tithed" twenty percent from his first art show (he's a painter), thirty percent from the next, and over fifty percent from his last show — just at the time he was trying to come up with the money for an engagement ring. Waxing theological, I attempted to explain that the tithe was technically ten percent, but he just shrugged that off in typical son-to-father fashion, "Yeah, yeah, whatever."

He told me that he had already had the big money discussion with Moriah. In Jonathan's words, "Yeah, she's crazy committed to a life of generosity too. I wouldn't marry someone who didn't have the same calling to give. Generosity is non-negotiable."

Margin and the Purpose of Money

Remember when you were learning to write with that fat pencil and horizontally lined paper? Your paper had one vertical line that was usually red. That line marked the margin, and everything to the left of that margin was off limits. You could only use the space to the right of the margin.

Now, let's think about margin lines in terms of time and money. I don't know how it is with you, but the older I get, the more things I seem to need and the less time I seem to have. This mystery of ever-increasing needs and ever-disappearing minutes makes the margin difficult to manage.

If every second of every day is tightly scheduled, then it takes a supernatural miracle of God for the Holy Spirit to break into our day and use us in unexpected ways. When we get so busy that we have no margin in our schedules, we pass ministry opportunities and human needs every day, and we don't even realize what God wanted to do in and through us. In the same way, if we live on the edge financially with little or no margin, we probably will not be looking for more opportunities to give. When we live without financial margin, we miss countless opportunities to invest, save, and give.

We are only aware of our opportunities to give and to serve in the context of the margin we create for ourselves. In other words, with no spare time for anything, we're unlikely to think too deeply about what we're called to do. And with no financial margin, we're unlikely to think too deeply about the meaning and purpose of our money.

The Hundred-Year Question

My good friend, Bishop Juray Mora, describes money as a *tool* God gives us to build people's lives and to advance His Kingdom. Juray points out that sadly, "Too many Christians have accumulated a nice tool collection, but don't actually use tools for God's intended purpose." How about you? Are you collecting tools or using your financial tools to honor God?

What will happen in the next one hundred years if we live like everyone else and only give God our leftovers? What will happen in Every Nation in the next one hundred years if we create financial margin in our lives so we can generously finance the advancement of God's Kingdom?

SEVENTEEN

DADDY, ARE YOU BLACK?

Diversity: unlikeness, multiformity, dissimilarity, variety.

I do not wish my house to be walled on all sides and my windows stuffed. I want the cultures of all lands to be blown about my house as freely as possible.
— Mahatma Gandhi

Before me was a great multitude that no one could count, from every nation, tribe, people and language.
— Apostle John (Revelation 7:9)

ELEVEN YEARS AGO, my friend Robert was at home in Manila watching a movie with his three-year-old daughter, Betthia. The movie, *Finding Forrester*, was about a brilliant, underprivileged African-American teenager who was being mentored by a reclusive Pulitzer Prize–winning writer played by Sean Connery. Great movie. Anyway, Robert told me that every time the movie featured a close-up of the young African-American actor, Betthia would look at the screen, then turn to him, then the screen, then him. Her head was turning back and forth like she was watching a tennis match.

After a couple of scenes, Betthia said, "Daddy, I have a question. Are you black?"

Robert smiled at his eldest daughter and replied, "Yes. And so are you."

Betthia immediately responded, "No, I'm not black. I'm brown, like Mommy."

Robert is what is known in the Philippines as a Fil-Am — half Filipino and half American. His dad, an African-American, was in the US Navy and stationed at Subic Bay when he met Robert's mother, who is a Kapampangan from Pampanga, Philippines.

Unity, Diversity, and Confusion

A similar question was asked by a curious five-year-old in Nashville who approached his mother and asked, "Mommy, are we black?"

Unlike Betthia, who has a multi-ethnic dad and a Filipina mom, this Nashville boy has two totally Caucasian parents, Rice and Jody Broocks.

Jody's answer was classic, "Wyatt, you'll have to ask your father."

Growing up in a multi-ethnic church, surrounded by Asians, Africans, Latinos, and Euros, Wyatt was momentarily confused about his own ethnicity. Diversity was his reality. And diversity is the Every Nation reality. Whether you're in Dubai, New York, Singapore, Toronto, London, or Johannesburg, you probably noticed that we're intentional and aggressive about diversity.

The same way Betthia and Wyatt inquired about family ethnicity, many times when people visit an Every Nation church they wonder if it's a black church, a white church, a Latino church, an Arabic church, or an Asian church. It's difficult to label us, because we embrace diversity as a key component of our church culture. Sometimes I forget that not everyone embraces diversity the way we do.

Bad Advice from a Good Pastor

I'll never forget the bad advice I received from a missionary-pastor of one of the largest churches in Manila. It was about fifteen years ago, and we were beginning to reach hundreds from Manila's Chinese community.

"Steve, if you keep reaching Chinese-Filipinos, you will have to start a separate Chinese service for them."

I tried to clarify. "There's no language barrier. They all speak English, so they attend the same service as the Filipinos."

Now it was his turn to clarify. "I'm not talking about language. I'm trying to warn you that if you mix Chinese and Filipinos, you will eventually have a church split. I'm speaking from experience. It will never work."

I'm glad I ignored his well-meaning but unbiblical warning. We now have thousands of Filipino-Chinese, Chi-Noys, Malaysian Chinese, Singaporean Chinese, and every other type of Chinese in our Metro Manila congregations. And we don't have a separate Chinese congregation or service. We are one church that is multi-site, multi-service, multi-generational, and multi-ethnic.

Every Nation Dubai has people representing over thirty nations worshipping together including Indians, Iranians, Sri Lankans, Filipinos, Nepalese, Nigerians, Kenyans, South Africans, Russians, Americans, and others. Every Nation London looks a lot like Every Nation Dubai. So does Every Nation New York and Every Nation Toronto. Every Nation Singapore includes almost every ethnicity in Southeast Asia, along with a few Aussies, Kiwis, South Africans, and Americans thrown in the mix.

Why do we intentionally and aggressively build multi-ethnic congregations? Here are two biblical reasons:

1. **Jesus died for everyone, not just for people like us.** If Jesus only died for Filipinos or South Africans, then I guess having a Filipino-only or South African-only church is okay. But, if Jesus died for every nation, every tribe, and every language, then shouldn't our church reflect that diversity? In Revelation 5:9, John writes, "You are worthy to take the scroll and to open its seals, because you were slain, and with your blood you purchased for God persons from every tribe and language and people and nation."

2. **Jesus called us to disciple every nation, not just our own.** In the past, in order to fulfill the Great Commission, people had to ride camels or board ships to get to remote nations. Today, the nations have gathered in major cities around the world, so it's possible to go to the nations without leaving the city. Some will need to actually leave and go, but many can "stay and go" because the nations

have come to us. Matthew 28:19 reads, "Go and make disciples of all nations."

Ethnic Diversity Is a Gospel Issue

Ethnic conflict is not a recent church problem. Two thousand years ago, the apostle Paul addressed racial segregation in his letter to the Galatians. I realize that along with the hypocrisy of racial segregation, Paul was also correcting theological and cultural issues in his epistle, but the racial issue was certainly part of the problem.

In the introductory pages of his commentary on Galatians, *Paul for Everyone: Galatians and Thessalonians,* N.T. Wright notes, "Imagine you're in South Africa in the 1970s. Apartheid is at its height. You are embarked on a risky project: to build a community centre where everybody will be equally welcome, no matter what their colour or race."

Wright's parable continues with the original builder leaving and a new group taking over. However, the new leaders are not committed to diversity. Eventually, the original project builder returns and is shocked to find that unity with diversity has been replaced with segregation.

According to Wright, this is the situation in Galatians. Paul, the Jewish apostle and his Greek assistant, Titus, started a church that welcomed Jews and Greeks. But after Paul and Titus left Galatia, the church forgot about its cultural value of diversity. Paul wrote the letter of Galatians, in part, to rebuke ethnic segregation and division. Notice the apostle Paul's strong views about diversity in the church.

- **Paul saw ethnic diversity as a Gospel issue.** Peter the Jew ate with Gentiles until other Jews arrived, then he only ate with Jews. Paul saw this as a Gospel issue, not a cultural or dietary preference. "We did not give in to them for a moment, so that the truth of the gospel might be preserved for you" (Galatians 2:5). "When I saw that they were not acting in line with the truth of the gospel, I said to Cephas in front of them all, 'You are a Jew, yet you live like a Gentile and not like a Jew. How is it, then, that you force Gentiles to follow Jewish customs?'" (Galatians 2:14).

- **God does not show favoritism.** At this point, some of the Jewish believers still thought that God liked them more than He liked the

Gentiles. "As for those who were held in high esteem — whatever they were makes no difference to me; God does not show favoritism" (Galatians 2:6).

- **The Gospel should be preached to all ethnicities.** "They recognized that I had been entrusted with the task of preaching the gospel to the uncircumcised [Greeks], just as Peter had been to the circumcised [Jews]. For God, who was at work in Peter as an apostle to the circumcised, was also at work in me as an apostle to the Gentiles" (Galatians 2:7–8).

- **Paul rebuked Peter for the "hypocrisy" of ethnic segregation.** This was no minor disagreement between Paul and Peter. Because it was a Gospel issue, Paul felt compelled to rebuke Peter publicly for his hypocrisy. "When Cephas [Peter] came to Antioch, I opposed him to his face, because he stood condemned. For before certain men came from James, he used to eat with the Gentiles. But when they arrived, he began to draw back and separate himself from the Gentiles because he was afraid of those who belonged to the circumcision group. The other Jews joined him in his hypocrisy, so that by their hypocrisy even Barnabas was led astray" (Galatians 2:11–13).

Why a Healthy Church Requires Diversity

I've spent most of my adult life as a white guy in a brown world — an American missionary in the Philippines. After twenty-four years living in Manila, Deborah and I now split time between Manila and Nashville, where Every Nation's North American office is located. As I have re-engaged American church culture, one of the more shocking experiences is the realization that so many churches are still basically white or black or Latino.

That's not good.

In the spring of 2012, I had the privilege of participating in the Lausanne Strategic Working Group in Orlando, Florida. I learned a lot from the forty brilliant strategists, theologians, and missiologists in the room. The meeting ended with an evaluation question: "What was missing that could have made this meeting more effective?" My answer required no deep thought or prayer. It seemed obvious to me that the missing ingredient was diversity. That Strategic Working Group was basically a room full of middle-aged, highly educated, white men — plus three Latinos, an Indian, a Korean, a Nigerian, and a Lebanese. Forty white dudes with a little color can create good strategy, but increase the diversity and the ideas go from good to great.

When the church gets serious about diversity, good things happen. "The color line was washed away by the blood." That's how Pentecostal historian Frank Bartleman described the early days of the Azusa Street Revival a century ago. During one of the most racist periods of American history (1890–1925), most early Pentecostal churches were bold exceptions to the culture of segregation. Sadly, it didn't take long for religious people to redraw the color lines that had been washed away by the blood.

In 1897, several years before the Azusa Street Revival, the Church of God in Christ (COGIC) became the first legally chartered Pentecostal church in America. COGIC founder C.H. Mason grew up hearing about the vibrant faith of Southern slaves from his parents who had recently been freed. He would build COGIC on the foundation of prayer, the power of the Holy Spirit, and racial unity.

For many years, COGIC had as many white ministers as black. Read that sentence again, and remember we're talking about one of the most racially divided periods in American history. This unity and diversity effectively ended in 1914 when most of the white COGIC pastors broke off to establish the Assembly of God (AoG). Undaunted, Mason continued to work on both sides of the racial divide, often speaking at AoG conferences for many years.

My favorite Mason quote is as true today as one hundred years ago: "The church is like the eye. It has a little black in it and a little white in it, and without both, we cannot see." Without racial diversity, the church cannot see. That explains a lot about the blindness in the church today.

The Hundred-Year Question

If we want correct vision and fresh revival, maybe we should take a page from the Azusa Street playbook and embrace unity with diversity. What will Every Nation become in the next one hundred years if we do not build diversity into our culture and only reach people who look like us? What will Every Nation become in the next one hundred years if we intentionally, aggressively, and strategically embrace ethnic diversity as a lifestyle?

EIGHTEEN

RADICAL OR REASONABLE?

Sacrifice: the surrender or destruction of something
prized or desirable for the sake of something considered
as having a higher or more pressing claim.

When Christ calls a man, He bids him come and die.
— Dietrich Bonhoeffer, Theologian and Martyr

I urge you, brothers and sisters, in view of God's mercy,
to offer your bodies as a living sacrifice, holy and
pleasing to God — this is your true and proper worship.
— Apostle Paul (Romans 12:1)

BELIEVERS FROM ALL OVER the world prayed as they followed the reports regarding the imprisonment and trial of my Iranian friend, Mahmoud. No one prayed more than Every Nation church members. Mahmoud first shared his story publicly at Every Nation's 2010 World Conference in Manila. For many of the twenty thousand in attendance, his testimony was the most unforgettable moment of the conference.

Three years before that conference, I was in Dubai having coffee with Mahmoud and other Middle Eastern believers. Mahmoud requested prayer, stating that police intimidation and threats had recently increased. He was planning to move with his family to another part of the city for safety. Before he was able to relocate, and within a few weeks of that prayer request, Mahmoud was arrested.

Facing the Death Penalty

After four and a half months of solitary confinement, intense inter-rogation, and daily threats, Mahmoud found himself standing in the highest criminal court in the Islamic Republic of Iran, facing charges for apostasy — a crime that carried a mandatory death penalty under Iranian law. At the end of the final hearing, Mahmoud was asked three simple questions by the Supreme Judge:

"Is your father a Muslim?"

"Yes, he was," Mahmoud answered, "but he died many years ago."

"Do you have fear of God?"

"I have," Mahmoud replied, "but I am praying that God will in-crease it in me."

"Do you want to submit yourself to the hand of God?"

"It is my prayer to know His will and to follow Him."

While the judge was clearly referring to the central tenet of Islam (submission to God), Mahmoud was referring to a decision he had made nine years earlier — one that had and would continue to guide his life. A Muslim for forty-three years, Mahmoud had never been in a Christian worship service until September 1999, when he inadvertent-ly caught the end of a service while picking up his wife from an Every Nation church meeting. She had recently begun attending church in the Middle Eastern nation where they were living at the time.

Mahmoud recounts, "I had been a cultural Muslim who denied that there is a living God because I didn't feel His presence. However, a month earlier at a Christian meeting, my wife had been miraculously healed from an illness."

That day in September, when Mahmoud visited his first church service, the pastor approached Mahmoud and asked if he could pray for him. With permission granted, the pastor laid hands on Mahmoud and began to pray.

"Something happened," Mahmoud says. "I felt something strange, something warm within me, and that night I made a simple decision. I had to know Jesus Christ, and I had to read the book which they call the Bible."

Mahmoud started attending church with his family, participating in Bible studies, and asking countless questions about Jesus. Within a month, he "discovered" that he had become a Christian. He explains, "Without intentionally wanting to change my religion, I felt deeply that I was in love with Christ. I felt that I was a new person who called Jesus 'Lord.' So, from that time on, I called myself a follower of Christ — a Christian."

Just Like the Book of Acts

Nineteen months later, while visiting Iran for his mother's funeral, Mahmoud and his family felt that God had called them to stay and share the Gospel with their countrymen. Here is how Mahmoud remembers those first few months back in Iran, as the new church emerged:

> Without having very much knowledge about church planting or evangelizing, the church was started with prayer — praying for our families, our relatives, our friends, and anyone who was in need. God's grace was with us . . . and from the very first steps, miracles happened.

A few weeks after moving to Iran, Mahmoud prayed for a relative who was suffering from a serious spinal condition that could result in paralysis. Within a few weeks, his relative was completely healed. A few months later, the relative and his wife and children became Christians — the first people added to their small house church.

Over the next seven years, many more were added to their number — more than three hundred Iranian Muslims received Christ, and more than two hundred of them were baptized. Of those years, Mahmoud recalls:

> There were so many miracles and so many signs and wonders that happened — things which we saw with our own eyes. If I were to tell them one by one, it would be a very thick book. Cancerous tumors shrinking, evil spirits departing, God speaking to many people in dreams and visions. It was just like the book of Acts.

Deny Christ or Die

With house churches now in five Iranian cities, Mahmoud traveled around Iran every week, encouraging and training new groups of believers. On May 15, 2008, while Mahmoud was meeting with disciples in a park in Shiraz, the Iranian secret police — known officially as "The Ministry of Information" — raided their meeting and arrested Mahmoud and some of the other disciples. Most were questioned and later released, but Mahmoud was kept in solitary confinement.

"I was interrogated for almost three months," Mahmoud recalls. "They were insisting that I repent and go back to Islam and deny my faith in Jesus. But I rejected their demands. In fact, I shared the Gospel with them."

In the third hearing, the judge, tired of Mahmoud's obstinacy, put the crime of apostasy on his file. Mahmoud explains, "This meant that I had lost my faith in Islam and that I would be considered an idolater. Under the new law, I would be subject to execution by hanging."

While in prison, Mahmoud worshiped, prayed, and fasted:

I deeply believed that my fellow Christians were praying for me and that the same miracle that happened in the book of Acts would happen to me — that somehow God would release me from the hand of the enemy. During the final hearing, I saw the miracle of how God changed the heart of the Supreme Judge.

The miracle came in the form of an unexpected verdict. After Mahmoud had answered the three questions, the Supreme Judge declared, "Even though you say you are a Christian, I believe that in your heart you are still a Muslim. You are released."

Immediately, an officer of the secret police leapt to his feet, pointed at the judge, and shouted, "You cannot do this! You are not allowed to release him! You are supposed to execute him! You must make an example of him!" The judge had made his decision, however, and Mahmoud was free to go.

Upon his release, Mahmoud and his family were kept under close surveillance by the Iranian secret police and were unable to meet with the other believers, for fear of compromising the other house churches.

Because of this, they left Iran and spent several years in different Asian nations while applying for United Nations religious refugee status. They then spent several years in the Philippines, studying at the Every Nation School of World Missions.

In 2011, Mahmoud and his wife moved to the United States, where he works with the mission department of Every Nation North America. Mahmoud now spends his time engaging Muslims with the Gospel and training churches to reach out to Muslim immigrants in their communities.

In 2007, when Mahmoud first informed me that he was being intimidated and threatened by the Iranian officials, he made it clear that he was ready and willing to sacrifice his freedom, his material possessions — even his life — for the sake of the Gospel. He was not looking for a way to avoid suffering, but for wisdom to continue ministry in the midst of persecution. To him, and to his Iranian friends, suffering and sacrifice is just part of following Jesus. To many of us, sacrifice is something we read about in history books, but not something that actually impacts our lives.

Persecution Is Part of the Package

During our 2012 Middle East Strategic Summit (MESS) in Dubai, our main topic was persecution. We studied what the Bible says about persecution. We prayed for the persecuted church. We heard accounts from Every Nation leaders who have suffered persecution. And we formulated a policy outlining how we would respond in the future when Every Nation people are arrested or face death in hostile nations. We asked hard questions about our willingness to give the ultimate sacrifice on the mission field. Everyone in that discussion had counted the cost and was ready to lay their lives on the line in order to obey the Great Commission. Yes! I get to work with some amazing people!

My friend Timothy Loh, Every Nation Malaysia leader, was a key contributor in this difficult discussion. He walked us through every chapter of the book of Acts, explaining that persecution and sacrifice was as much a part of the early church as evangelism, worship, preaching, and miracles. I don't know how many times I've read and studied

Acts, but until this teaching, I had never noticed how much persecution was recorded in Acts. Almost every chapter featured arrests, beatings, threats, warnings, prison, prison breaks, and more beatings.

Through all the threats and persecution, the early Christians continued to boldly preach the Gospel of Christ. And new churches were planted despite the religious and civil persecution.

Here's a quick ten-point summary of Timothy's teaching on persecution and suffering:

- Persecution was common in the New Testament.

- Persecution followed the preaching of the Gospel.

- Persecution came from religious and civil authorities.

- Persecution often involved imprisonment.

- Persecution was usually violent.

- Persecution sometimes resulted in death.

- Persecution accelerated the spread of the Gospel.

- Persecution prompted prayer for boldness, not prayer for protection.

- Persecution resulted in rejoicing.

- Persecution never stopped or hindered the mission of the church.

Today, we see persecution as abnormal and unfair. The early church saw it as normal and unavoidable. In addition to the book of Acts, most of the epistles address persecution. Notice what Paul writes in 2 Timothy 3:12: "In fact, everyone who wants to live a godly life in Christ Jesus will be persecuted."

According to Paul's letter to Timothy, we don't even have to do a good job of living godly. In fact, if we so much as desire to live for God, we will be persecuted.

Suffering for Christ — Radical or Reasonable?

I remember my first trip to China over twenty-five years ago as quite an adventure. It felt a bit James-Bondish. Along with a few Filipino pastors, I smuggled Bibles across China's border and secretly delivered them to couriers who, in turn, delivered them to pastors in China's rural areas. Our training was intense, our mission was eternal, and our cargo was priceless. By accepting those smuggled Bibles, our Chinese contacts were risking years of imprisonment. Our risk? Being yelled at and sent back to Hong Kong.

Many have suffered and much has changed since my first trip to China. Each time I return, I'm impressed by all that God is doing in a land that has tried so hard to keep Him out. As I taught a group of fifty Chinese pastors recently, I felt compelled to say, "Years ago, thousands of pastors and missionaries traveled to China from all over the world to smuggle Bibles and teach the Chinese church. In the coming years, thousands of pastors and church leaders will come to China from many nations, not to teach, but to learn from the Chinese church."

They seemed puzzled as to why Christians would come to China to learn from them. In their minds, they'd simply responded to the Gospel by giving the Lord back all they had. They never really thought about all they had sacrificed to follow Christ. I tried to explain that as people who have endured persecution without compromising their faith, they have much to teach believers who serve God in comfort and safety. I'm still not sure they understand how much they have to offer the rest of the world, but I know that those of us who live with religious freedom have much to learn from those who have sacrificed so much for their faith.

I remember a conversation I had with Mahmoud a few years after he was released from prison. We were sitting in the safety of my Manila office. As we discussed his time in prison facing the death penalty, I heard not one word of regret or uncertainty about why God allowed things to be so difficult for him and his family. Instead, he talked about his suffering as a *gift* from God, merely his *reasonable service*. To him, prison and persecution were nothing radical, unusual, or unexpected — just part of following Jesus and carrying a cross.

Mahmoud's reasonable attitude was nonetheless astounding to me. It was reminiscent of William Borden's legacy I wrote about in chapter 16. While many might have considered Borden's sacrifice to be a great waste — dead at the age of twenty-five — he did not. Remember his final words, scribbled on a piece of paper: "*No reserve; no retreat; no regrets!*"

I see that same attitude, commitment, and response from people in nations hostile to the Gospel. I also see it in the Bible. The apostle Paul wrote to the church in Rome, "I beseech you therefore, brethren, by the mercies of God, that you present your bodies a living sacrifice, holy, acceptable to God, which is your *reasonable service*" (Romans 12:1 NKJV).

Many preachers challenge their congregations to "make radical commitments" to Christ. I've probably said it myself many times. But the willingness to lay it all on the altar is not really radical. In view of God's mercy, it's a reasonable sacrifice.

The Hundred-Year Question

We're called to every nation. We have already planted churches and campus ministries in most of the safe, comfortable, and easy nations. The dangerous, difficult, and closed nations await us. Much sacrifice will be required to finish the Great Commission.

What will Every Nation become in the next one hundred years if we choose security and refuse sacrifice? What will happen if we only go to the easy and open nations? But, if we are willing to sacrifice comfort, safety, and security and go to *every* nation, what might God do in and through us in the next one hundred years?

ACKNOWLEDGMENTS

I've been asked how long it takes to write a book. The actual writing of *100 Years from Now* only took five months, January through May. But learning and living the principles took at least twenty years, from the day Every Nation started until today. Writing the book required some help. Living the principles required even more help. I owe thanks to many people for helping me learn, live, and write these truths:

- To Every Nation's co-founders: Rice and Phil, thanks for believing in me and for believing with me.

- To Every Nation's Asia team: Jackie, Joey, Jun, Larry, Manny, Michael, Sam, Scott, Simon, and Timothy, thanks for continuing to include me, even when you don't need me.

- To Every Nation Campus Ministries' global leaders: CJ, Joe, Nick, and Olajide, thanks for following, and thanks for leading. Our future is in good hands.

- To Every Nation's Manila office: Ado, Carlos, Jiji, Pinky, and the team, *maraming salamat.*

- To Every Nation's Nashville office: Bill, David, DeNail, Justin, Kevin, and the team, *Thanks, y'all.*

- To the book team: Walter, thanks for helping me clarify, simplify, and record the vision so runners can run. It's a privilege to work, think, and write with you. Let's do this again some time. Bruce, Noel, Paul, Winston, thanks for the biblical and theological input and adjustments. David, Joel, and Dunham Books, thanks for your professionalism and excellence.

- To the family: William and Rachel, James, Jonathan and Moriah. Thanks for keeping me grounded in reality, and for reminding me of what really matters. Deborah, thanks for everything, really, everything. My name is on the cover, but the ideas, stories, and scars are ours.

ABOUT THE AUTHOR

Steve Murrell is the co-founder and president of Every Nation Churches & Ministries, a global movement of churches focused on church planting, campus ministry, and world missions.

In 1984, Steve and his wife, Deborah, went to the Philippines for a thirty-day mission trip that turned into thirty years and counting. They are the founding pastors of Victory Manila, one church that meets in fifteen locations across Metro Manila, and that has planted churches in sixty Philippine cities and twenty nations. Today, Victory has more than eight thousand discipleship groups that meet in coffee shops, offices, dormitories, and homes throughout Metro Manila.

Steve is the author of *WikiChurch* and coauthor of *The Purple Book,* a foundational Bible study with more than eight hundred thousand copies in print. It has been translated into twenty-two languages.

Steve serves on the board of the Real Life Foundation, a Christian nonprofit that seeks to provide underprivileged Filipino youth with a better future by transforming their communities and giving them access to a good education.

After living in the Philippines for twenty-four years, the Murrells now split their time between Manila and Nashville. Their three adult sons were born and raised in the Philippines and now reside in the United States. When in Nashville, Steve serves on the leadership team of his local church, Bethel Franklin.

For more information, blogs, and podcasts, visit stevemurrell.com.

EVERY NATION

Every Nation is a worldwide family of churches and ministries that exists to honor God by establishing Christ-centered, Spirit-empowered, socially responsible churches and campus ministries in every nation.

Since it was established in 1994, Every Nation has been making disciples, training leaders, and planting churches all over the world. Our vision is to see a multi-ethnic, multi-generational Church that will seek first the Kingdom of God for the glory of Jesus Christ, about whom it is written: "With your blood you purchased for God members of every tribe and language and people and nation" (Revelation 5:9).

For more information about Every Nation and its work around the world, please visit our website or social media sites.

Every Nation Churches & Ministries
P.O. Box 1787, Brentwood, TN 37024-1787 USA
Tel +1-615-371-8479   E-mail info@everynation.org

www.everynation.org